W9-DBO-586

LOVERS

New male-female sexuality will be as effortless, unself-conscious, and playful as sex between two people who just want to be next to each other. The quality and ease of their experience will be stimulated by each other's presence.

The new male-female relationship will be a fluid interaction between two total people, each capable of a full range of human responses. They will come to lovemaking for no other reason than a genuine desire for closeness.

THE NEW MALE-FEMALE RELATIONSHIP

"FASCINATING!"—*Pacific Sun*

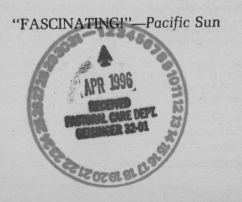
APR 1996
RECEIVED
PASTORAL CARE DEPT.
GEISINGER 32-01

More Reading from SIGNET and MENTOR

(0451)

☐ **IT CAN HAPPEN TO YOU: The Practical Guide to Romantic Love by Dr. Roger Callahan with Karen Levine.** Forget the excuses—give love a chance. If you think you are amoro-phobic—afraid of romantic love—this practical and realistic workbook, filled with quizzes and gidelines, will tell you exactly what your fears mean, and how you can free yourself to fall in love and love every minute of it. (122704—$2.95)*

☐ **HOW TO BE AN ASSERTIVE (NOT AGGRESSIVE) WOMAN IN LIFE, IN LOVE, AND ON THE JOB—A Total Guide to Self-Assertiveness by Jean Baer.** Are you a portrait of a "lady"—or are you a person? Learn how to express your opinions and wishes, and stand up for your rights with these revolutionary new techniques of assertiveness training by the co-author of the bestselling *Don't Say Yes When You Want to Say No.* (125827—$3.50)

☐ **THE CHALLENGE OF BEING SINGLE: For Divorced, Widowed, Separated, and Never Married Men and Women by Marie Edwards and Eleanor Hoover.** Here is the book that gives fresh and important momentum to the singles revolution as it shows the exciting growth and fulfillment staying single can offer both men and women. (099036—$2.95)*

☐ **FOR YOURSELF: The Fulfillment of Female Sexuality by Lonnie Garfield Barbach.** Here is a unique book that demonstrates in a step-by-step program how you can indeed take control of your life at its most intimate, personal and fundamental level—to achieve orgasm and a greater fulfillment of your sexual potential. (119479—$2.95)

*Prices slightly higher in Canada

Buy them at your local bookstore or use this convenient coupon for ordering.

THE NEW AMERICAN LIBRARY & COMPANY
P.O. Box 999, Bergenfield, New Jersey 07621

Please send me the books I have checked above. I am enclosing $_____
(please add $1.00 to this order to cover postage and handling). Send check or money order—no cash or C.O.D.'s. Prices and numbers are subject to change without notice.

Name_____

Address_____

City _____ State _____ Zip Code _____

Allow 4-6 weeks for delivery.
This offer is subject to withdrawal without notice.

THE
NEW
MALE-
FEMALE
RELATIONSHIP

HERB GOLDBERG, Ph.D.

A SIGNET BOOK

NEW AMERICAN LIBRARY

PUBLISHER'S NOTE

In all of the case histories cited here, with the exception of those involving public figures, the author has used fictitious names and described traits not identifiable as those of any particular person or persons.

NAL BOOKS ARE AVAILABLE AT QUANTITY DISCOUNTS
WHEN USED TO PROMOTE PRODUCTS OR SERVICES.
FOR INFORMATION PLEASE WRITE TO PREMIUM MARKETING DIVISION,
NEW AMERICAN LIBRARY, 1633 BROADWAY,
NEW YORK, NEW YORK 10019.

Copyright © 1983 by Herb Goldberg, Ph.D.

All rights reserved. No part of this book may be reproduced or utilized in any form or by any means, electronic or mechanical, including photocopying, recording, or by any information storage and retrieval system, without permission from the publisher. For information address Sanford J. Greenburger Associates, Inc., 825 Third Avenue, New York 10022.

Published by arrangement with
Sanford J. Greenberger Associates, Inc.
A hardcover edition was published by
William Morrow and Company, Inc.

SIGNET TRADEMARK REG. U.S. PAT. OFF. AND FOREIGN COUNTRIES
REGISTERED TRADEMARK—MARCA REGISTRADA
HECHO EN CHICAGO, U.S.A.

SIGNET, SIGNET CLASSIC, MENTOR, PLUME, MERIDIAN and NAL BOOKS
are published by New American Library,
1633 Broadway, New York, New York 10019

First Signet Printing, July, 1984

3   4   5   6   7   8   9

PRINTED IN THE UNITED STATES OF AMERICA

FOR Lois and Amy

Acknowledgments

After completing this book, I thought about how fortunate I was to be living in a time and a society where the reexamination of traditional, time-honored, sanctified beliefs and assumptions about the male-female relationship is possible. Rather than viewing the old days with nostalgia, I perceive them as having reduced the male-female relationship to a level far below its potential. Therefore, I feel greatly indebted to all of the psychological, social, and liberation pioneers who broke down the barriers to make it possible for us to live the human experience more creatively and authentically.

Specifically in regard to the writing of this book, I wish to express my gratitude to my editor, Maria Guarnaschelli, whose guidance, attention to detail, and encouragement pushed me to produce a more cohesive book. Rita Monroe, who helped me in organizing materials and typing the many revisions of this manuscript, was invaluable because of her relaxed, incisive, patient, and intelligent assistance. Thanks also to Jim Landis of William Morrow and Company, who has been continually supportive of my work and who generates a personal, attentive atmosphere in an often impersonal industry. Finally, my appreciation to Francis Greenburger, who placed this book with the two fine publishing houses of William Morrow and Company and The New American Library.

—Herb Goldberg
December, 1982

Contents

Introduction

FAILURE in the traditional male-female relationship is psychologically built in the inevitable. Still, when relationships deteriorate and shatter, self-hating feelings of personal inadequacy and failure arise. Neurotic conflicts, immaturity, couple mismatch, and fear of commitment are commonly blamed. The implication is that once one has resolved these personal problems, good relationships will become possible.

This book will explain the many ways that gender conditioning, which is the psychological process by which the male and female learn to be masculine and feminine counterparts, makes enemies of men and women. As a result, "love" turns to hate, or at best is transformed into a stagnant impasse wherein two people remain in a relationship laden with compulsive, ritualized behavior, sundry psychological and physical symptoms, and guilt.

Masculine and feminine conditioning has also turned the course of the male-female relationship on its head. Most couples bond in romantic euphoria, evolve into a deadened interaction, and separate with feelings of alienation and sometimes concealed rage or open hatred.

What we call masculinity and femininity are psychological defense systems that distort and repress the critical human feelings, needs, impulses, and processes required for healthy consciousness and personal development. These defenses produce a man-woman attraction based on fantasy and the incompleteness of each partner, which dooms the relationship to stagnation and rigidity at best, failure and building fury at worst. *The rescuer becomes the jailer.*

Today, the rage that accumulates behind the docile feminine mask has surfaced directly via feminism. The women's movement did not create this intense anger, but rather channeled it and gave it expression. This has resulted in the emergence of many women who are defensive toward men, despise them, or lack the ability to give or receive love in relation to them.

However, the tendency of some women to blame men for their problems shows clear signs of abating. Women's consciousness seems to be arriving at a broadened awareness that both sexes have been locked into a mutually reinforcing dance in which there are really no victims or victimizers, only the illusions of such.

I believe that the social movements we have called women's and men's liberation are eruptions caused by the pain, anger, and fear produced by gender conditioning. They are manifestations of the need to throw off the shackles that have severely damaged the desire and ability to relate intimately to the opposite sex.

The nostalgia expressed by some for the old forms is self-deceiving. The relationships of the past never really worked to the benefit of both partners. At best, they were functional adjustments, compromises, or accommodations to social pressure.

While divorce and the instability of relationships are a troubling part of our present, I believe we stand on the brink of a totally new consciousness in regard to the male-female relationship. With greater psychological awareness and freedom from gender defensiveness, our relationships could enter a process of expansion and mutual freeing-up. As people grew older in them, they would assimilate the kind of self-awareness that results in growth, increased playfulness, expressiveness, and genuine intimacy.

This book is the last in a trilogy. My first book on these issues, *The Hazards of Being Male*, explored the psychological underpinnings and self-destructiveness of traditional masculinity. *The New Male*, which followed, defined the newly evolving male consciousness and its relationship to the emerging female one. *The New Male-Female Relationship* examines the foundations of the traditional relationships that produced anger, frustration, and fear of intimacy. It then explores the transitional path away from the past, and the potentially even more damaging binds and traps that come into being when people begin the complex process of extricating themselves from the strictures and structures of yesterday. This is a time in which intellectual awareness and liberated attitudes are prone to be in conflict with deeper emotions and needs, which makes the male-female relationship even more fragile, if not impossible to maintain. Guidelines to facilitate a constructive transition period are offered here. Finally, the book defines the new male-female relationship, which will be characterized by a rooted playfulness with authentic friendship, companionship, and sexuality.

I feel a personal sense of urgency in writing this book. The old roles have become too poisonous for any truly conscious and sensitive person to accept. A new blueprint is a necessity lest men and women cement themselves into hardened postures of mutual antagonism and alienation. As people in a world that has put a premium on technological development rather than human growth, and as individuals who look to intimate relationships as the source of our deepest satisfactions, we are entitled to the pursuit of a new and better personal vision.

PART ONE

TRADITION

1 The Machine and the Child

THE TRADITIONAL male-female relationship is a relationship between a machine and a child. The more closely she resembles the feminine ideal, the more childlike the woman is psychologically. The more accurately he approximates the masculine ideal, the more machinelike the man is in his behavior and consciousness of himself and his life. The relationship between the two produces guilt and hopelessness in the male, and feelings of rage, helplessness, and victimization in the female.

Both have expectations, of themselves and each other, that are psychologically impossible to meet, and that therefore give rise to a sense of failure and personal inadequacy. Because of the perpetuation of relationship myths, men and women alike are haunted by the feeling that something is wrong with them, when actually failure is built into the basis and structure of these relationships. Those that survive it or, seemingly, succeed in it do so largely by denying and submerging their inner experience in obedience to their roles. A rare few find genuine and mutual satisfaction, because they have managed to free themselves from the defensive strictures of masculine and feminine role defensiveness.

We have paid the price for this impossible dream with the growing breakdown of the male-female relationship. Traditional masculinity and femininity produce people who have a distorted awareness of the world and of their emotions, impulses, and bodies. This leads naturally to the destruction of the relationship.

He is a machine, driven by the unending need to prove himself. Therefore, he lives by acquiring symbols that validate him, rather than by experiencing the process of his life. His is motivated by how things make him look as a man, not how they actually feel. As a result, he loses his capacity for human connection and intimacy.

The male's strength is an illusion, built on the defensive belief that he can transcend humanness to become a well-oiled, perfectly functioning machine. A self-made business tycoon and athletic champion described his life thus: "I'm running so fast, I'm gonna burn myself out." He then reflected on his own father: "He decided when he was about seventeen, that he was going to be a millionaire when he was thirty. He didn't accomplish it until he was fifty. When he achieved his dream, he was dead by his own hand two years later. He told me, when I was twenty-four, 'Don't ever set your goal. Don't let your dream be something you can accomplish in your lifetime.' "[1]

Not all male machines can even justify their dehumanization with the rewards of wealth, power, or fame. Most are machines because that's all they really know how to be, even if it is destroying them in the process.

Asbestos workers, for example, are in a high-risk occupation, and often their payoff is disease and death. Said one union leader, "There was one day I woke thinking, 'Gee, we work with this stuff and it's killing us.' I could never believe it. . . . Even when my friends started dying, it was hard to accept." He added, "I can't admit that I could die from it. I've seen the terrified looks when they got ill. One fellow had cancer. When he found out, he wouldn't go back to the doctor. He died a few months ago. All he ever said was, 'The only thing I can do is cover pipes.' "[2]

The writer of a book on living without working in a "nine-to-five world" described his experience with his father this way: "One night, ten years ago, my father was complaining about his job. After 40 years of selling women's hats on the same street in Manhattan, the pay was still lousy, his boss didn't give a damn about him and nobody bought hats anymore. . . . That night, I wanted to say something because I knew time was running out, that every morning he had to put a nitroglycerin tablet under his tongue to make it up the subway steps with his sample case. So I offered him some money and suggested he take time off to relax. . . . 'I can't quit,' he said. About a year later, he died."[3]

While the male is transformed into a machine, the female remains in a childlike state. Feminine conditioning stunts her so that she will not, perhaps cannot, use her potential power and strength directly to function autonomously, decisively, and by taking direct responsibility for the shape of her life and her experiences. For decades, American films have made the love goddess a child-woman. From Clara Bow to Lillian Gish, Mary Pickford, Shirley Temple, Jean Harlow, Marilyn Monroe, and Brigitte Bardot, the message is clear: baby talk, a pouty manner, and cooing helplessness are the techniques that make a sex goddess. Forever children, these love queens are worshiped for being infantile, helpless, emotional, weak, clinging, and compliant. Rescuing and protecting them allows the male to "feel like a man."

Author Una Stannard summed it up: "The woman [is] forced to remain a charming, dependent child. . . . Woman's mask of beauty is the face of the child, a revelation of the tragic sexual immaturity of both sexes in our culture."[4]

Clare Boothe Luce, former congresswoman, also described the state of femininity well:

> Now consider how the average little girl is brought up in middle- and upper-class America. She is generally led to believe that she can remain a child (a sheltered dependent) her whole life long, on one condition: that she find a "good man," i.e., a substitute for Daddy, to marry her. This husband-daddy, she is told, will give her a real doll's house to "play house" in, with real furniture in it, and a real range to cook on, and best of all, he will give her real live dolls— babies—to play with. Early in life she is taught to think of herself as a housewife and to expect that as a housewife she will "belong" to her husband, just the way she "belongs" to Mom and Daddy. She will let him decide what is best for her in all

important questions. And if she is a good little Big Girl, who gives him his way in all the big things, she can have her way like Mom in all the little things. And Mom will show her how to tease, pout, cry, and coax him in such a way that only little things ever come up. As for love, well, if she just stays pretty and sweetsmelling, soft, yielding, and submissive (feminine), she will be loved by her daddy-husband in that special way in which grown boys are permitted to love grown-up little girls. All this, and sex too! Marriage— wow! Childhood plus if you can get it.

... The Venus image, the Love Goddess, "Oh-you-beautiful-doll" erotic image of woman has been similarly reinforced by the media. Endless commercials and T.V. programs show the lovable woman as a cuddly, soft, yielding girl-child sex object, with hair that bounces, teeth that invite deep kisses, a body that smells like Heavenly Spring. The message is that woman is a creature intended by nature itself to be endlessly made happy by being showered with goodies and gifts from her husband or lover (clothes, jewels, cars, etc.).[5]

WOMAN: WHAT FEMININE SOCIALIZATION DOES TO HER

Her Assertion Complex

The author of a self-assertion guide for women wrote, "The woman in our society who conforms to the traditional feminine role is basically a nonassertive person. In social situations, she finds it difficult to express negative opinions or to set limits against the intrusion of others on her time and energy. She expresses emotions but not strong opinions. She is intuitive, not analytical. She underemphasizes her accomplishments. She maintains 'an attitude of frail dependence on men.' "[6]

That frail dependence leaves her feeling unsure of herself, uncomfortable making decisions, and with the deeply frightening sense of having no identity of her own. She comes to feel that she is not a person and that she is not taken seriously. She is a boring companion because she has difficulty defining personal preferences and passions, and she comes to blame the man in her life for having deprived her of identity. The blaming has a hollow ring, however, because even when encouraged and supported by him in her desire to be assertive, she continues to react passively, being unable to clearly define herself and her preferences, and even becomes angered by the pressure on her to *act* rather than *react*.

Painful symptoms of her repression of assertion include a sense of being exploited and controlled, a strong desire to fuse her identity with a man's, feeling lost without him, and psychosomatic complaints such as chronic fatigue, headaches, and other pains that express her resentment at being controlled.

Her Aggression Complex

To be feminine is to be "sweet," "nice," "cheerful," "friendly," "compassionate," "kind," and without "an angry bone in her body." In short, it is to deny aggression.

The more feminine a woman is in this way, the more hopeless the prospect of true intimacy with a man becomes, because conflict between the two, when it occurs, can never be negotiated and resolved successfully. The repression of her aggression causes her to view herself as a victim. In any argument or fight, therefore, she tends to see herself as blameless and cannot own up to her part of the problem.

Generally, her response to an argument is fourfold. She cries, blames, withdraws, and then punishes by withholding affection. This usually incites guilt in her affection-hungry husband, who apologizes in order to make up, only to face another, similar, but even more agonizing round of arguments soon after. The rhythm of the relationship is endless and frustrating: painful fights followed by sentimental, short-lived reconciliations.

Her underlying aggression emerges in unmanageable, passive, indirect ways. Forgetfulness, procrastination, misunderstanding, saying the wrong thing at the wrong time, lateness, nagging, withholding affection, depression, moodiness, listlessness, compulsive mothering and homemaking, sexual manipulation, blaming and inciting guilt, acting helpless, being unpredictable, religious fanaticism, mysticism, self-righteousness, and even a nervous breakdown all may be expressions of it. Once she decides to get a divorce, the full force of her rage often emerges directly. Then she can be remorseless in her desire for retribution for all her years of being a "victim."

Her smothered aggression also causes her to be excessively fearful in social situations. She exaggerates the threat of such situations, overestimating the strength of others and underestimating her own. She is damaging to the man she is involved with in needlessly encouraging him to fight for her and over her. In that sense, the more feminine she is, the more dangerous she potentially is to men. The weaker the man perceives her to be, the more he will feel compelled to be aggressive, to "defend" her, and to prove himself in order to keep her love. Often this translates into senseless, violent, and self-destructive confrontations with other men over minor incidents, and taking on excessive burdens and challenges.

On an abstract level, however, she sees the world in an unrealistically optimistic, naïve way ("People are nice," "The world is a loving place"). Her femininity requires her to be seen as "sweet," "nice," and well liked. She unconsciously avoids perceiving and immersing herself in "harsh" realities and expects protection from the male.

In addition, she displays an endless array of physical ailments because her passivity makes it difficult for her to maintain her physical health, and because her repressed aggression can use this as a substitute way of gaining control. At the same time, these ailments silently express her resistance and anger.

The myth of the nonaggressive woman, the "sweet angel," is surely one of the most lethal for men. Relationships with her are stagnant, frustrating, unpredictable, and ultimately violent.

Her Autonomy Complex

Just as ideal masculinity translates into militant independence, ideal femininity involves clinging dependency, helplessness, and the search for a "strong" man to "take care of me."

The more helpless a woman feels, the more will she be attracted to a man based on his power symbols. Falling in love will be accompanied by baby talk, childlike admiration of his strength, an infantile desire to be held and "snuggled," and the use of affectionate names such as "baby." She will find it increasingly difficult to know who she is and what she wants. Particularly when she's in a relationship, she will tend only to react, and to fuse her own identity with the man's. She will engulf her male partner because of her need to compensate for her underlying feelings of helplessness. Inevitably, rage will build within her over feeling controlled and being treated like a child, with no awareness on her part of how she helped set it up that way. When she suddenly demands autonomy and freedom, it will have an adolescent flavor. That is, her motivation will be to rebel against her husband, the authority figure.

The degree of her feelings of dependency and lack of personal power directly determines the amount of anger that will build within her over being controlled, even though her anxieties about being independent cause her to be attracted to dominant, powerful men and to play a childlike role. *These feelings develop regardless of how well or badly she is actually treated.*

In extreme cases, depression, suicide, and the tragedy of spouse violence can result from this deeply rooted feminine dependency. Severe spouse violence rarely occurs without an extended prior history of lesser incidents of physical abuse. The woman often fails to leave the relationship because of her feeling of helplessness and fear of being on her own. The rage that builds up behind her dependency is manifested in indirect provocations, blaming, and emotional volatility. Her relationship with her husband will alternate between childlike clinging

and periodic eruptions of hatred. A pattern of
relationship brinkmanship will develop, as dependency and rage become equally and precariously
balanced.

Her Sexuality Complex

The feminine woman is sensual, not sexual. She
wants to be held more than to have sex. One married
woman spoke of her disgust and feeling of being
cheapened when her husband would ask her during
intercourse, "Isn't this a wonderful fuck feeling?" A
woman learns as a little girl that sex is nasty—
something men manipulate women to get, and
something women grant as a gift and use as a source
of power to control men.

The fact that she is not truly sexual is seen by the
fact that she can do without sex for long periods of
time if the man or the situation does not please her.
Sex is not her driving need. Her dominant need is
to be "loved."

Because she does not take direct responsibility for
her sexuality, she comes to feel used by her man,
and to see men in general as sexual exploiters. She
is "at his service" because sex occurs at his initiation
and she does it to please him.

In some cases, she comes to hate men for their
"animal impulses," to view them as rapists, and to
develop psychosomatic illnesses in order to avoid
sexual contact. She may also develop physical
oversensitivity and experience pain during sex.
Naturally, the more femininely passive she is in
bed, the more likely she will find sex painful and
feel she is being handled too roughly.

Her Rationality Complex

The counterpart to masculine repression of emotion is feminine repression of the rational side. A traditionally feminine woman tends, therefore, to be credulous and mystical in her way of perceiving things. The more feminine she is, the more she is drawn to superstition, gurus, astrology, religion, and development of a personal sense of moral superiority. She is also vulnerable to manipulation by charismatic leaders, "healers," and doctors.

In relationships, she resists logical exploration of issues and tends instead to overemotionalize in the face of a conflict. "I don't care whether it makes logical sense or not. It's just how I feel," she will say. The rational resolution of problems therefore becomes impossible.

In moments of crisis, she tends to fall apart, crying and screaming. She resists developing competence with finance, business, machinery, politics, and systematic long-range life planning. Tending to avoid responsibility in these matters, she then finds herself resenting her vulnerability and the feelings she has of being treated like a child and being "kept powerless."

MAN: WHAT HIS MASCULINE DEFENSES DO TO HIM

His Dependency Complex

In masculine consciousness, dependency and need are equivalent to weakness. The underlying fear of being dependent walls in the traditional man and isolates him. He has difficulty articulating his real needs and fears, and asking for help. He comes to feel uncared for, unknown, and cynical about relationships because he can't be real and be himself in them; he can't feel safe even with his supposedly closest intimate, his wife.

His resentment over feeling uncared about and having his unspoken needs unfulfilled emerges in countless indirect forms, including withdrawal and nonresponsiveness, criticism and sarcastic humor, passive indifference, insensitivity, workaholism, and even self-destructive behavior like alcoholism, reckless driving, and gambling, which damage his family as well as himself. At the same time, he comes to see his rewards in life as opposite to what he anticipated. In spite of doing all the "right" things, he feels unloved, dissatisfied, like a failure.

He relies totally on his relationship with his wife because she is his sole intimate involvement, and although he becomes deeply dependent on her, he rarely recognizes it. He likes to feel that he doesn't really need anybody. When his wife does suddenly leave, however, often he collapses. His independence then is seen for what it is: a pose that is both brittle and superficial.

His Fear Complex

Fear equals femininity. To be fearful is to be a sissy. Masculinity means transcending fear. The less fear this kind of man experiences, the more manly he sees himself as being. The need to overcome fear often leads to self-destructive actions. He throws himself into situations and accepts challenges that endanger him and that he is frightened of, in order to prove to himself that he is not afraid, or that he can defy fear.

His defensiveness against fear muddies his ability

to perceive his real feelings. When he experiences inner resistance, his major motivation is to prove to himself and others that he is courageous and unafraid, and therefore he ignores fearful feelings.

The potential destructiveness of this need can be seen metaphorically in famous daredevil circus performer Karl Wallenda, who died of a fall during his act. One magazine reader commented, "Would the Wallendas' seven person pyramid have been any less magnificent with a net? Would crossing a wind-swept street on a high wire require any less skill with a net?"[7]

His Passivity Complex

To the traditional male, passivity equals femininity, while activity means masculinity. Therefore, the more active he is, the more masculine he feels. He may in fact become compulsively active. Sleeping is seen as an unmanly waste of time. He has difficulty recognizing and giving in to tiredness. Transcending fatigue validates him. Therefore, the more closely he approximates the masculine ideal, the more likely he is to physically burn out prematurely. He lacks pacing, and a recuperation cycle to balance the intense activity.

His is a driven personality. The high rate of heart attacks and hypertension among men may reflect, in part, the overstress of constant activity without due recognition of fatigue. A man can be deeply tired without knowng it, or giving in to it. To overcome it, and to make up for the human stimulation he's not getting, he doses himself with cigarettes, coffee, liquor, a high-protein diet, and excitement.

His Emotions Complex

A man-machine conducts his life in a defensively cerebral way. Emotions are seen as weaknesses, and are therefore repressed. This makes him extraordinarily competent with the mechanical aspects of life, but stupid, vulnerable, and often a victim of his own blindness in intimate relationships. He fails at his attempts to conduct his relationships by means of rules and intellectualization. He often cannot differentiate a genuine response from a manipulative one. His relationships break down without his understanding why.

His woman leaves and he didn't know she was unhappy. His children feel alienated from him though he gave them his "best." He has no close, intimate friends of either sex. He is successful in the world, but humanly isolated.

He is the victim of psychosomatic disorders such as ulcers and back problems, stemming from the repression of feelings of dependency, fear, resistance, and so on. His moods swing constantly and uncontrollably. He is a numbing, unsatisfying friend because he is insensitive to the emotional and interpersonal aspects of a relationship and his conversation is therefore impersonal, boring, indeed deadening.

His Sensuality Complex

He is sexual but not sensual. He wants sexual relief, but is uncomfortable with non-goal-directed holding and caressing. Consequently, he approaches sex mechanically and eventully turns off his partner. Sex in a relationship becomes work, rather than play. Sexual pleasure is severely limited because he experiences sex as an act, not as a part of being close.

Extensive touching makes him uncomfortable. Being touched by a man is intolerable, and by a woman it is not meaningful, comfortable, or satisfying it if does not relate to sex. Even then, he cannot handle very much of it.

The more masculine he is, the worse he is as a lover, despite his sexual illusions about himself and his quest to be a superperformer, because he is uncomfortable with playful, sustained sensuality and is insensitive to emotional cues. Therefore, his sexual relationships inevitably deteriorate and begin to irritate and repel his woman, thus becoming a source of anxiety to him.

His Femininity Complex

Anything that suggests the feminine threatens him and makes him uncomfortable—women's activities, interests, jobs, attitudes, and even clothes, colors, drinks, food. That is, he won't wear certain colors because they are feminine, nor will he drink or eat certain beverages or food that he considers to be for women only.

Closeness to other men on a warm, affectionate basis is a threat because it implies homosexuality. His relationships with other men are therefore competitive, distant, unsatisfying; they only intensify his loneliness and dependency on the woman in his life.

The more he fears being feminine, the more fixated he is on masculine symbols, e.g., guns, cars, motorcycles, football games, and liquor. As a result, there is almost no basis for any real sharing and connection with his woman; and the more feminine the woman—his romantic ideal—the more this is true.

Researcher Evelyn P. Stevens writes cogently of the defensive masculine style: "Because the fear of losing his potency is ever present, the macho lives in a nightmare world; like a writer between books, or an actor between plays, he is desperately unsure about whether he can produce another hit. . . ."[8]

His Submission Complex

His equation of submission with weakness and unmanliness means he can only relate and connect comfortably when he is in control. He will risk life and health when only his masterful self-image is at stake. His need for control in his close relationships—with his woman, his children, and others—causes him to be resented and even hated. Even in his "benevolent" moments, when he believes he is giving to others generously, anger builds toward him because others feel patronized, condescended to, and controlled.

The fear of submission also translates into a competitive compulsion to win. It creates a grim seriousness, even when he's "playing," that infects every interactive experience. Therefore, there is no relief for him in games. Everything becomes a variation on war. He is resentful when he loses and resented when he wins. Eventually, it becomes more draining and unpleasant for him to engage himself socially than to isolate himself.

He hates losers and he hates himself when he loses. Since losing becomes more likely as he gets older, feelings of self-hate and failure are built in to his life experience.

His Proving Complex

Masculinity is a draining, lethal, and insatiable defensive process. Everything a man strives to prove he is not, actually he is. He basically identifies with women because his earliest imprinting and socialization as a child was largely through his mother, grandmother, and other female relatives, teachers, and nurturers. Therefore, his masculinity is, in many ways, a hollow defensive posture.

The internal experience of one highly successful businessman, age forty-nine, thrice divorced, vice-president of a major corporation at the time he wrote this, illustrates the consuming, constricting, and frustrating results of this proving complex:

> I have to keep proving that I'm better than other men. It's never good enough to be just as good as other men. I must get rid of competition and must prove that I'm better every day, all the time. I can't stand to compete with other men. I must keep aloof and above them.
>
> I only function sexually with a woman when I'm the only one. But then I get possessive and fearful that I can't fulfill all of her needs and that I'm not perfect.
>
> Even amongst my competitors in business, I'm very aloof and snotty. I don't want them to get close. I don't want to come down to their level for fear I'll be just one of the boys and get swallowed up, consumed, laughed at, or beaten.
>
> I don't want to get close. I'm actually embarrassed about myself and all of these feelings. Therefore, I try to be better and appear superior. But inside I'm lying to myself.

I want the confidence of being no better and no worse than the next guy. I'm tired of being angry all the time, defending myself against my feelings of being no good. The slightest thing that goes wrong evokes anger, because the going wrong means that I'm no good!

Being alone is confirmation that I'm NO GOOD!

Not having someone to love is a feeling of being NO GOOD!

Being poor and unsuccessful is being NO GOOD!

Being late, held up in traffic, delayed, encumbered, not having the answer, not being as I think I'm supposed to be is NO GOOD!

As long as I think I have to be super special, better, superior, I'm going to lose. Every moment of every day I'm trying to prove this. How do I lose my desire to fulfill the fantasy of being superior so that I can come down to earth and enjoy myself? The desire to fulfill the fantasies of being better makes me run and search, twenty-four hours a day. I can't stop long enough to love myself and appreciate myself and my accomplishments and my own humanness.

BREAKING DOWN

Countless studies by psychological researchers have demonstrated a direct relationship between traditional masculinity and femininity, and the presence of anxiety and low self-esteem and acceptance.[9]

The consequences of this gender socialization process, in which boys are conditioned to be masculine and girls to be feminine, are already manifested early in life. The prevalent behavior of young boys and young girls is a compelling variation on the typical characteristics of masculine men and feminine women.

Male children have a four- to eight-times-greater incidence than females of infantile autism, hyperactivity, and contact disorders.[10] These disorders can be seen as extreme developments of normal or even lauded masculine traits. That is, autism is a pathological resistance to human attachment and emotional connection, often accompanied by a fixation on mechanical objects. It resembles the obsession of grown men with their automobiles, television sets, and gadgets, men who are uncomfortable in person-to-person involvement.

The hyperactivity syndrome involves an uncontrollable tendency to be in motion and unable to slow down. Again, this can be seen as a variation on the behavior of the adult male who has to always be doing something and who prides himself on his "endless" energy and ability to go on little sleep.

Females beyond puberty have a two- to four-times-greater incidence than males of depression and social phobia.[11] Depression has been shown to be related, at least in part, to an inability to express aggression directly and fully. It is also known to be the result of learned helplessness and feelings of being powerless to control one's life. The female's significantly higher rate of social phobia is an outgrowth of her difficulty with assertion, aggression, sexuality, and independent strength. The more feminine she is, the more will people and life in general become a source of fear and intimidation.

When the machine and the child begin to unravel as adults and have breakdowns, their experiences will be predictable as direct outgrowths of their separate defense systems.

According to psychiatrist Peter A. Martin, this is a common pattern for women at the time of a marital breakdown:

> The wife comes for treatment first because she has been experiencing severe anxiety, depressions, or incapacitating physical symptoms. . . . She claims that her sickness is due entirely to the coldness and cruelty of her husband. She insists that he does not care about what she wants or what she feels. She states emphatically that she has a deep capacity to love, but that her husband is cold, unsympathetic, cruel or psychotic. . . . She complains that her husband is either sexually inadequate or oversexed. She blames her sexual unresponsiveness on her husband. . . . To her, the only solution is a change in her husband.
>
> Their relation to their husbands is of a symbiotic, parasitic type. They suffer from the narcissistic problem of low self-esteem. They do not experience a fixed, firm, stable personality of their own as distinct from the need-satisfying object. . . . [12]

In her novel *The Bell Jar*, based on her own life, Sylvia Plath, a renowned writer and herself later a suicide, describes the breakdown of the heroine, Esther. It is a tragic variation on the pathology emerging from the traditional feminine consciousness.

Esther hears from her boyfriend's mother that "what a man is, is an arrow into the future and what a woman is, is the place the arrow shoots off from."[13] The cause of her problems is the feminine conditioning that denied and degraded her total personhood. She is obsessed with the feeling that others will notice how stupid she is, and will be repulsed by her hairy legs and general ugliness.

In the process of trying to find the ideal man, who will love and rescue her, the same thing continually happens. "I would catch sight of some flawless man off in the distance, but as soon as he moved closer I immediately saw he wouldn't do at all."[14] Her endless struggle to find her identity is expressed through her constant self-assuring inner refrain "I am, I am, I am."

When the breakdown of a woman is accompanied by the direct acting out of rage toward her husband in the form of murder, it is with a guiltless sense of righteous anger. In *A Staff Report to the National Commission on the Causes and Prevention of Violence*, sociologist William Goode wrote, "Wives rarely commit suicide after committing homicide; the combination most often carried out by males. . . . The husband is more likely to feel guilt and remorse than wives do."[15]

The symptoms of a woman's emotional breakdown are but a logical extension of her femininity: a sense of having no identity ("I don't know who I am or what I want"), blaming rage toward the man in her life, depression and feelings of helplessness, a host of psychosomatic symptoms, feelings of sexual repulsion and/or extreme frigidity, and a sense of confusion that makes her almost immobile.

When the male breaks down, his symptoms too are the inevitable outcome of his conditioning. The details are, however, more difficult to see and explore because he is embarrassed by weakness and so resists asking for help, is unable to readily perceive and articulate his deeper feelings, and tends to self-destruct through alcohol or direct suicide rather than express his conflict, rage, and pain openly.

Nevertheless, the portrait of a traditional man in the process of breaking down would probably include:

- Feelings of extreme isolation and loneliness; a sense that nobody gives a damn about him.
- Fear of opening up lest he be seen as cowardly, weak, or a burden on others.
- Intense guilt about a multitude of things, in addition to feelings of being a failure.
- Great anxiety about his sexual capacities, adequacy, and performance.
- An attitude of extreme cynicism and despair.
- Physical debilitation, alcoholism, chain smoking, and so on. His physical condition, because of his distorted macho health consciousness, is badly damaged. He has stomach problems, hypertension, back problems, or overall enervation, and can't sleep or go to the bathroom properly.
- Hopelessness about ever getting help or effecting any change. He is resigned and feels defeated.
- Self-condemning inner ruminations, such as: "My life is going nowhere."
  "I haven't got enough money to do the things I really want."
  "Other men are passing me by."
  "If I had only tried harder when I had the chance."
  "I am inferior."
  "I am unlovable."
  "I've destroyed everything that I've touched."
- Finally, bitterness because the promised rewards of being successful and living up to masculine expectations did not materialize. Indeed, he feels further away than ever from leading the life he

envisions for himself. If his wife has left him, he may see no reason to continue. He feels his children hate him and condemn him for all of the family problems. "They'd all be better off without me," he tells himself.

HIS "FEAR" OF AND HER "DESIRE" FOR INTIMACY

In the traditional depiction of the male-female relationship, the man is seen as fearing intimacy and loss of control, while the woman is seen as having a great capacity to commit herself, to love, and to be intimate.

Viewed, however, from the perspective of their conditioning, it becomes clear that neither the man nor the woman has the capacity for genuine intimacy. His "fear" of it and her "desire" for it are both distortions based on their gender conditioning and expectations. He fears losing control by getting close because he is subconsciously aware that he will be engulfed by her needs and the pressure to perform and take care of her, and will feel guilty if he fails.

In the process, he will lose the edge of excitement he originally had in the relationship, which was provided by distance and a sense of challenge. His resistance to intimacy and marriage is, therefore, healthy self-protection.

Likewise, her desire to be intimate cloaks her deeper sense of helplessness, repressed aggression, dependency, and anxiety about experiencing untrammeled sexuality. *What she really wants is not intimacy, but the fulfillment of her need to define her identity through him, to be taken care of and protected, and to have her sexuality legitimized by a "committed" relationship.*

Her capacity for real intimacy, therefore, is no greater than his; it simply has the appearance of being greater. The result of all this, however, is that the male is left with guilt, self-doubt, and self-hatred as he accuses himself and is accused by others of an inability to be loving; while the woman is left feeling frustrated, deprived, and resentful over her inability to find the deep, meaningful relationship that she imagines she wants and believes is available to her somewhere.

THE REAL DIFFERENCES BETWEEN MALE AND FEMALE

We are born male and female. We are socialized to become masculine and feminine. The common contention that the differences between men and women are deeply rooted in genetics and biology derails us from an awareness of how we prevent little boys and little girls from expressing their humanness to the fullest. If indeed we are programmed genetically to be masculine and feminine, then the programming is enormously damaging psychologically to men and women, and we need to question and work toward altering the destructive course we are on. Indeed, *a "healthy" relationship of genuine intimacy and growth becomes impossible in direct proportion to the degree a couple fits the ideal models of masculinity and femininity.*

The artifacts of conditioning known as masculinity and femininity can be seen as defensive reactions against oneself, because they often produce a sudden, dramatic reaction to the other extreme.

Mr. Autonomous emerges as a clinging, desperate baby.

Miss Helpless announces that no one will ever again control her.

Mr. Decisive is paralyzed with indecision.

Mrs. Sweetness becomes a raging fury with a guiltless capacity for homicide against her husband.

Mr. Animal Sex becomes unable to get an erection and is terrified by intercourse.

Ms. Passive, once divorced and on her own, works full-time, goes to school, raises her children, and juggles several lovers.

Mr. Autonomy won't let his wife out of his sight and doesn't want to go on when she leaves.

Mrs. Dependent says, "I just need to be alone."

The defensiveness of masculinity and femininity produces a rigid balance between men and women, making change frightening and painful. It is, therefore, less threatening to rationalize that we are products of biological inevitability than to experience the anxiety and chaos involved in the process of growth.

A world of "machos" (masculine males) and "earth mothers" (feminine females), however, is a world that keeps both sexes at a low level of human potential, causing men to be overtly self-destructive and women indirectly so. It distorts body (health) consciousness, makes the sexual experience stressful and threatening, and produces feelings of rage and helplessness in women and guilt, failure, and self-hatred in men. It blocks change in relationships and distorts the capacity to be aware of reality. It encourages parenting by unprepared, infantile men and women ("babies having babies"), turns men into machines, stunts women at the child level, and vastly accelerates the death process.

2 The Myth of Intimacy: Love Turning to Hate

WE HAVE CHASED the illusion of intimacy; we have become embittered at our inability to make love work; and we feel betrayed by the opposite sex. The very best intentions and efforts have too often proven futile. Caring has too often turned to apathy, while passionate love has been transformed into rage.

We have all been victims of the unconscious processes that are part of the romance of masculine-feminine relationships. Genuine intimacy will emerge only after these processes have been defined, acknowledged, and rooted out, so that men and women will no longer be trapped by images, symbols, gender defenses, and the actor-reactor imbalance.

How often has the tragedy been played out? Two people who believe they have achieved a deep and meaningful relationship see it dissolve into feelings of alienation and hatred. Couples drawn together by the strongest loving commitment and sexual passion end their relationship in total estrangement, unable even to speak together or tolerate each other's presence. Even for those who did endure out of habit, fear of the unknown, economic necessity, or resigned acceptance, the underlying feeling is transformed from passionate love to hostility and even contempt.

It has been called "the war between the sexes," or "the longest war." It is the traditional relationship, which has turned many contemporary women into man-haters. Articulated repeatedly by feminist writers, the attitudes are variations on a familiar theme. Women feel they have been abused, exploited, raped by men, and conned into being nice with the lie they would thus get what they wanted. But all it seemed to bring was pain.

Shakespeare expressed this age-old pessimistic theme through the voice of Hamlet, speaking to Ophelia: "If thou dost marry, I'll give thee this plague for thy dowry: be thou as chaste as ice, as pure as snow, thou shalt not escape calumny. Get thee to a nunnery, go: farewell. Or, if thou wilt needs marry, marry a fool; for wise men know well enough what monsters you make of them. To a nunnery, go, and quickly too. Farewell" (act 3, scene 1).

Whether the feelings are manifested as rage, as hate, as a defensive self-containment and distrust designed to keep all heterosexual intimacy at a distance, or simply as burned out apathy, there is a sense among many contemporary people of being defeated in their ventures into intimacy, and great wariness about further attempts at commitment.

The tragedy, of course, is that while men and

women end up seeing each other as sources of pain, betrayal, and fear, at some earlier time the same relationships that now embitter them brought them to the highest peak of joy and the deepest well of trust and caring.

What went wrong?

LOVE TURNING TO HATE: THE CAUSES

Because the process of socialization that turns the male into a masculine man and the female into a feminine woman destroys significant capacities and potentials in both, much of what attracts each to the other is illusion. The strong, fearless man and the lovely, delicate woman—the romantic ideals—are manifestations of their gender defenses rather than true expressions of their full being. Men and women are drawn to each other to compensate for the limitations created by this socialization process, and then are wounded or destroyed by the rigidity and defensiveness existing behind the seductive facade.

Both "fall in love" with the projected defenses of the other and then later come to feel repelled and limited by the very traits they were drawn to initially. The impulse to grow and change in one becomes a threat to the security of the other. Hence, one's orginally loving, supportive partner becomes the enemy who blocks expressiveness and change.

She to Him

She is attracted to his independent, self-contained way of being because it reassures her that he is strong, manly, "his own person." Later in the relationship, she comes to resent him for being distant and invulnerable. It makes her feel frustrated about "really" getting close. She feels unneeded and unable to understand what it is that he wants.

His rational, level-headed approach to people, situations, and problems is attractive in the early stages of the relationship. She gets a sense of comfort and solidness from the fact that he never seems to get flustered or to let emotions get in the way. *Later in the relationship*, she comes to resent him for being cold, closed ("I never know what you feel"), insensitive, and "always so damn logical." She complains that he seems unable to respond to her spontaneously or to show emotion.

Initially she is attracted to his sexual urgency. His seemingly ever-present physical need makes her feel sexy, desired, and reassured about her attractiveness. *Later in the relationship*, she comes to be turned off and even repelled by what she sees as his selfish, crude approach. She feels used and becomes sexually defensive because, according to her, he treats her like a sex object, is insensitive to her needs, and only touches her when he wants intercourse.

Also, she is attracted to his ambition, his competitive attitude, his drive, and even his self-serving cynical opportunism, which initially amuses her. She believes she understands him. She feels reassured and protected because of his goal orientation and his sense of discipline about work. *Later in the relationship*, she comes to resent him for his seemingly endless obsession with his job and pursuit of money, his lack of playfulness, and what she now perceives as his egomaniacal need to accrue power and success. She feels neglected, bored, and resentful because, according to her, all he thinks or really cares about is his work.

When they first met, his aggressive, outspoken,

gutsy, even pushy style excited and intrigued her. Also, she felt protected by his seemingly fearless attitude. *Later in the relationship*, she comes to see him as insensitive, too direct, immature, belligerent, reckless, irresponsible. It makes her feel threatened, frightened, and embarrassed.

Likewise, his active style and enthusiasm for doing things and going places is attractive in the beginning. She is stimulated by his exuberance and endurance. *Later in the relationship*, she comes to see him as restless, tense, and unable to relax. She says she feels drained and pressured because he always has to be doing something and going somewhere, and because he seems to grow bored so readily.

Finally, his dominating manner makes her feel secure initially because he's a "real man" whom she cannot manipulate, while he can master her. *Later in the relationship*, she becomes outraged by what she feels is his condescending, chauvinistic, controlling attitude. She feels put down and militantly informs him, "Men cannot do what they want with women!"

He to Her

He is attracted to her emotional intensity, her ability to readily express love and other feelings, and her volatile but vulnerable quality. Her expressiveness makes him feel connected to her and very much alive and human. *Later in the relationship*, these same qualities are proof to him that she is irrational and unable to control herself. He grows progressively more exasperated by her emotional outbursts and frustrated about trying to "talk sense" to her.

Her seemingly great need for him and that innocent, helpless quality initially make him feel needed and manly. *Later in the relationship*, he comes to see her as dependent, childlike, and demanding. He feels oppressively laden with responsibility and guilty whenever he cannot immediately fulfill her wishes or is not there when she "needs" him. He feels he has been dragged into a bottomless well of needs and wants.

He is drawn to her "sweetness" and "niceness." She seems to have infinite patience, great compassion, and a positive outlook on people and life. Her kindness makes him feel accepted, less cynical about life, more loving. *Later in the relationship*, he comes to see her instead as naïve about people and life. It irritates him and causes him to act in a paternalistic way as he tries to teach her about "harsh realities." He is increasingly unwilling to trust her with the responsibilities he would like to give up himself.

Initially, he is taken by how easy she is to get along with and how positively she reacts to his suggestions and plans. Her agreeable and accommodating personality makes him feel validated, appreciated, understood, and supported. *Later in the relationship*, he comes to see her as lacking in identity, insecure, and confused about who she is and what she wants. He feels bored and bewildered because of her lack of input ("I don't know what she really likes"), and guilty when things go wrong because he was the one who made the decisions.

Her inhibited sexual manner when he first dates her reassures him. He is comforted by her insistence that sex is only meaningful within a loving and committed relationship. It feels good to believe that she's "a lady," that she's not cheap or easy. *Later in the relationship*, he comes to feel that she lacks real sexual drive, and that she's doing him a favor when she has sex with him. He feels frustrated by her seeming lack of spontaneous passion, and his sense of being responsible for turning her on. Often, he feels he is intruding on her when they have sex and comes to resent her for her apparent lack of any strong sexual desire.

Initially, her tendency to be physically passive, her noncompetitive, uncoordinated attempts at sports ("She looks so cute"), and her indulgence in sleeping late, or sweets or eating out are seen as a part of her special charm. Her lack of physical agility and interest in athletics or staying in shape reassures him of her femininity and makes him feel strong and superior. He even likes teaching her about sports. *Later in the relationship*, he comes to see these same qualities as meaning that she is lazy, negligent about her physical health, and a poor partner in sports due to her seeming lack of drive and competitive spirit.

LOVE FREEZES OVER

In general, all the qualities that are initially so attractive become offensive because they are not full, spontaneous expressions of the person, but rather expressions of defenses. *And, because these initially attractive masculine and feminine qualities are defensive, they are rigid.* It is attractive for a woman to have a loving, positive attitude toward the world if she can also respond appropriately to its harshness and dangers. Likewise, it is reassuring to see a man with intensity, ambition, and courage, if he can also be playful, relaxed, and comfortably able to accept failure, and can engage others in a noncompetitive way as well as a competitive one.

Furthermore, the defensive repressions in the feminine woman dictate that her man remain forever the way she believes he is. That is, if she fears being aggressive, assertive, decisive, or directly sexual, she will need to have him compensate, filling the vacuum she creates in the relationship. He must remain permanently fixed in his masculine posture in order to balance her. Her initially attractive qualities end up becoming obstacles to his growth, because he cannot let go of his defensive responses once the balance is established and he has assumed the responsibility in certain areas for both of them. This also promotes his self-destructiveness, as he winds up killing himself in his unending compulsion to fulfill the manly role.

His rigid need to be in control and to prove himself by being the protective doer and decision maker blocks her attempts to be assertive and autonomous. She is forced to be femininely submissive in the extreme, and a crisis arises when she endeavors to become strong and to take charge of her own life. Therefore, her "loving" man inevitably becomes an obstacle to her growth.

Often, the entire basis for the relationship is a balancing act, each person compensating for the deficiencies of the other, and as either one begins to become whole, the very foundations of their relationship may begin to disappear because they have nothing else in common to hold them together. Any change in one person, therefore, becomes a threat to the other and will be met with resistance.

Indeed, once locked into a relationship, the balance between the two people may be so sensitively tuned that the slightest change in either one sets off a cataclysm. The more extreme the polarization and, therefore, the more "romantic" the couple, the more rigidly balanced they are and the less play or tolerance for change there is. Thus the high-intensity romance transforms itself into stagnant boredom. It is as if one partner or both were hanging on for dear life.

THE PREMARITAL, POSTMARITAL REVERSAL

Once the battle to win the other person has been won and he or she has been "secured," the need to be perfect disappears and the realization of being trapped into predictable, limited ways of living sets in. Underlying resentment over the disappointment and loss of self in having accommodated and having been accommodated begins to seep in.

This anger, and an unconscious desire to punish the other because of his or her fear of loosening up, may be manifested in a premarital, postmarital reversal in behavior. The opposite of what was there during courtship may begin to be acted out. The man who previously was the goer and the doer begins to become more passive and withdrawn. His urgent sexuality diminishes significantly and his independence becomes a string of childlike demands to be fed and attended to, with a tendency to always be at home underfoot. Many wives complain because their husbands have no friends and seem always to be around.

The woman who was once so supportive, warm, and kind begins to become critical and nagging. She gains weight and comes to bed without regard to being attractive. Her submissiveness becomes bossiness, while her demure sexuality grows into either coldness or a complaining demand for orgasm and extended loveplay that he cannot fulfill. It is as if she were taunting him as revenge for her disillusionment and sense of having lost herself to him.

By the time of the dissolution of the relationship, a total reversal may have occurred. She has become aggressive, angry, critical, militantly independent, defensive against anyone controlling her, sexually charged, and insistent that no man will ever again get close to her or control her. Meanwhile, he has become a vacillating, dependent, unsure, emotionally volatile, irrational, sexually intimidated, fearful person, easily controlled by the woman.

The rigidity of both their defenses was such that no flow could occur to improve things. Indeed, because the original bond was based on each person's defenses, or image as a man or woman, rather than on genuine, person-to-person knowing and liking, when the relationship starts to dissolve there are no loving threads to rebind it. The loved one is now seen as the enemy. "You made me miserable." "You fooled me into thinking you were someone you weren't." "You nearly drove me crazy." Attempts at reconciliation fail because one or both fear being seduced back into the original status quo.

His romantic self and hers were, to a great extent, opposite to what actually existed within each of them. Therefore nothing turned out as they imagined it would. Ex-lovers often have the sensation of being a total stranger to the one they "loved," once the relationship is terminated. Indeed, strangers they were.

ATTRACTION TO SYMBOLS: ANOTHER REASON LOVE TURNS TO HATE

To bolster his masculinity, the man makes his woman into a *sex object*. To compensate for her fear of independence, aggression, and the direct expression of power, the woman treats her man as a *success object*.

The more completely masculine and feminine the man and woman are, the more they need to depersonalize the opposite sex and perceive them in terms of symbols rather than as people. Mr. Macho (the masculine ideal) sees all women as breasts, legs, and faces, because his woman's features symbolically validate his masculinity. Miss Earth Mother (the feminine ideal) wants to know what the man does for a living and what his power (status and money) symbols are. Recognizing this, each uses these symbols to snare the other.

Both are attracted to *how it looks or what it does for them to be with the other, rather than how it feels*. Were either to stop at any given moment of their interaction to ask how it actually feels, the answer would be that it feels dead or boring. The *"excitement" they initially experienced came from basking in the warm, safe light of the other, from having won a prize, from being validated, rescued, and made to look good.*

The difference between a "symbolic" experience and a more genuine experience can be seen, for example, in a party at an enormous mansion with food and wine flowing and the guests dressed to the hilt, but all of them self-conscious about their image and tightly controlled about what they say; versus a party at a small apartment with simple refreshments and entertainment, and with guests who are playful, open, connected to each other, and unconcerned about status or image. The first party has the symbols, but not the process. It looks good, but it doesn't feel good to be there. The second has the process, but not the symbols. It is therefore experienced in a pleasurable and fulfilling way.

Because the man and woman each develop on some level a sense of being used by the other, underlying rage will build up, to the extent that each comes to feel dehumanized or treated like an object. Indeed, in such classically "romantic" couples, one or both inevitably end up feeling exploited for their function, rather than related to as a person. Each, however, tends to blame the other while forgetting that he or she helped to bring it on.

THE ACTOR AND THE REACTOR: PROCESS DESTROYS CONTENT

It doesn't really matter how nice you are or how hard you've tried. This is the painful lesson learned by many in traditional relationships who did everything "right" and still saw their relationship deteriorate. Commonly, when relationships break up, the tendency is to look for a cause, someone or something to blame.

The blaming orientation is the traditional one. Reasons are sought and latched onto as justifications. "He neglected her." "She let herself go." "They couldn't agree on money." "He had an eye for women." "She got tired of being his slave." "He drank too much." "She wanted a career." On and on.

In these instances, one or the other is depicted as

the heavy. Usually the one blamed most is the *actor*, who in most cases is the man, though where women have assumed the actor role they stand to be blamed. The actor is blamed because he is seen as responsible. It is the actor's part to initiate—to be directly sexual, decisive, aggressive, strong, and protective. In most relationships, the woman is the *reactor*. She waits for the man's moves and then reacts.

The courtship ritual is a cogent example. Men are traditionally responsible for making the first approach to a woman, initiating conversation, asking for her telephone number, calling for a date, driving the car, selecting the restaurant, paying the check, deciding on the entertainment, making the initial sexual overture, turning the woman on sexually, and even continually pursuing the relationship. Throughout, the traditional woman mainly reacts.

Since actors initiate and take responsibility, they feel guilty when things go wrong. Though reactors avoid this guilt, the price they pay is the loss of their identity. To the extent that they are reactors, they also feel controlled. To the extent that they allow themselves to be controlled, they feel put upon and build up rage. It doesn't matter how "nicely" they are treated by the man. Having no sense of being somebody in the relationship causes them to hate the actor, whom they see as their manipulator or oppressor, the person to blame regardless of the specifics of their interaction.

Rage actually builds on both sides. She, as the reactor, feels controlled and used. He, as the actor, feels trapped by responsibility and therefore doomed to be the bad guy when things go wrong.

This is a potent reason for the war between the sexes. Reactors experience this rage directly, and overtly blame the actor. Actors build unconscious rage only, because of their feeling of responsibility. But their anger comes through in periodic tirades about their seemingly endless burdens.

The process, meaning how two people interact—who is acting and who is reacting, whose identity is dominating and who is being passive and controlled—inevitably transforms and destroys the content, or what the words and deeds are.

It doesn't really matter how patient, knowledgeable, well intentioned, or kind either is, or whether they are Ph.D.'s in psychology or spiritual saints. The estrangement and anger will grow to the extent that there is an actor-reactor imbalance, so that one feels primarily responsible and the other feels primarily controlled. It is misleading, therefore, to pinpoint "causes" of a couple's problems—who did or said what to whom—and then try to resolve specific issues. Unless the actor-reactor imbalance is altered, a relationship cannot lastingly be improved.

A FORMULA FOR SPOUSE VIOLENCE

Powerful romantic feelings are frequently only a step away from painful explosions of rage, and the same defensiveness that produces romantic ardor also sets the psychological stage for such explosions, including spouse violence. This latter is rooted in the intertwining of powerful needs with feelings of being trapped and the hunger for freedom.

Those who would turn the tragedy of spouse violence into an issue of sexism, politics, or morality; who perpetuate myths about the brutalizing male and the "helpless" female; who make judgments about right and wrong; who define "victims" and "victimizers" do great damage to the process of growth and self-awareness for both men and women. Such an orientation reinforces alienating distortions that further the rift between the sexes.

Karen Coleman and Paula Howard of the Texas Research Institute of Mental Science did a study of wives who reported that they had been slapped, punched, and kicked.[1] Twelve percent had been beaten severely during pregnancy. Among their conclusions were:

1. Abused wives tend to define themselves totally by their relationship.
2. The majority of the women reported that they felt themselves to be independent and self-reliant.
3. The husband in such a relationship relies on the wife as his major source of psychological support.
4. There is, on both sides, a desperate desire to maintain the relationship.
5. The tenacity of couples in maintaining their chaotic, violent relationships is discouraging. Progress in therapy is slow and the dropout rate high as couples alternate between separation and reconciliation.

Bruce J. Rounsaville of Yale University studied thirty-one battered wives and concluded that the important feature characterizing wife beating is the intense and exclusive dyadic system in which the couple is enmeshed. While as an individual the man may not be violent, just as the woman is unwilling to tolerate abuse, once they are in the relationship a dynamic is created in which violence occurs.[2]

Barbara Star, a researcher at the University of Southern California, compared battered and nonbattered women and pointed to passivity rather than masochism as the key factor underlying the endurance of physical abuse.[3]

Based on her work with battered women at a southern California shelter, she concluded that the victims are "the most isolated group of women I've ever seen. . . . They have few friends and a terrible sense of insecurity. They're afraid to be alone." Their husbands "have deep feelings they can't express. Such men have rigid role expectations. They know what their wives should do and what to expect from themselves as husbands and fathers. Their views are inflexible, and when the stereotype isn't lived up to, the man often can't control his emotions. . . . While he explodes, the woman keeps her anger inside and often talks suicide." Star concluded, *"Yet the man and woman are people with basically similar personalities"* (italics added).[4]

Dr. Rodney J. Shapiro of the University of Rochester reported that "I have seen many families in which women have been beaten by their husbands. . . . I have never yet seen a family in which a woman was simply a victim and had no input in that behavior."[5]

These researchers are all telling us the same thing: spouse violence is a relationship problem and a two-way street, rather than a brutal male act that appears in isolation from the way a particular man and woman relate to each other.

Violence *by the wife* toward her husband has also been studied. One report, from researcher Murray A. Straus of the University of New Hampshire, about

2,143 couples, revealed that 11.6 percent of the husbands and 12.1 percent of the wives reported one or more physical attacks by their spouses within a one-year period.[6]

According to the deputy district attorney in charge of Los Angeles County's Child Abuse and Domestic Violence Unit, approximately 15 percent of spousal assault victims in 1979 and 1980 were husbands, and of the thirty-five hundred cases prosecuted or investigated annually, an estimated 10 percent of spousal attacks are against husbands.[7]

Spouse violence is the product of an interaction between two people who are intensely dependent on each other and feel trapped, frustrated, and disappointed at the same time. These feelings, inevitably generated in a polarized relationship, make the relationship a tinderbox. In some cases the anger emerges directly as physical violence. More often, in more controlled and "civilized" relationships, the rage is expressed indirectly or contained as previously described—via coldness, passive and indirect aggression, compulsive rituals, psychosomatic and emotional disorders, hurtful verbal encounters, and so forth. In the long run, these are probably equally damaging, only in different ways.

THE SPECIFIC INGREDIENTS THAT PRODUCE SPOUSE VIOLENCE

In all of these interactions, no one is to blame; everyone is a victim of a process they don't understand and can't control. The ingredients that set the stage for the rage that produces physical attack include:

1. A traditional woman whose childlike dependency and feelings of helplessness make her crave reassurance, contact, and closeness in a relationship with a machinelike male whose tendency is toward isolation ("Leave me alone") and who has minimal tolerance for emotional and personal interaction. A vicious circle is created as she demands more "intimacy" while he wants less. He walls himself off as she becomes more desperately insistent on contact in an infantile, persistent way. While she complains of rejection, he complains of being smothered.

2. A man and woman who are unable to fight fairly and resolve conflict. She expresses her growing anger in irritatingly passive and hidden ways such as nagging, flirting, and blaming, while he handles his anger by coldly withdrawing, criticizing, and attempting to control his partner even more by withholding whatever she needs.

3. An actor-reactor imbalance that is basically boring to both, though neither has the resources to effectively change things. They cling to each other even while the hunger for excitement and being with others grows in each of them. Mutual provocation expresses their unconscious wish to push away their partner.

4. A man and woman who are drawn to each other by defensive needs and insecurity and become excessively dependent on each other, while at the same time there is a latent hunger for further individual growth. The partner is

simultaneously needed and resented as an obstacle to freedom and personal development.

5. A man and woman who resent basic aspects of each other (for example, he may say, "You're too dependent on me") but are threatened by any changes their partner might attempt to make to improve matters. They continually block each other's growth in spite of expressed dissatisfaction with the way things are, and it becomes a no-exit, no-hope matter.

6. A cycle in which the same basic fights repeat themselves over and over again. The intensity of rage and frustration increases, however, because of the grinding-down impact of the repetitions. Both feel abused, maligned, unheard.

7. A man who has needs, but is unable to ask for what he wants and resents it when his wishes are not being correctly divined; and a woman who needs power and autonomy, but feels unable to directly take them and blames her husband for controlling her.

8. His increasing perception of her as a child who is irrational and insatiable; and hers of him as a machine who is withholding, insensitive, cold, and unreachable.

9. A woman who knows what she doesn't like, but has difficulty defining what she does want. She therefore responds negatively to her man, who is overly sensitive and readily irritated by her complaints of dissatisfaction because he feels responsible and guilty.

10. A relationship that begins on a tremendous romantic high with expectations that can-

not be maintained, and therefore generates feelings of disillusionment and of having been fooled.

Any one of a number of triggers can send these couples, who are nursing these painful feelings and conflicts, into a physical confrontation that temporarily releases the rage and produces the distance that neither can establish in healthy, open, and productive ways.

THE GROWING FEAR OF EACH OTHER

With each succeeding generation, the repressed rage between the sexes intensifies, producing a self-protective, phobic orientation. The fear of getting close is at the same time the fear of being destroyed and the fear of one's own destructive feelings toward the opposite sex. Relationships, therefore, tend to become increasingly more superficial, temporary, exploitive, and unsatisfying between men and women whose primary energies are going toward defensive maneuvers. Few relationships seem to maintain themselves without various powerful, indirect ways of creating a safe distance. In extreme cases, some men and women lose their capacity for heterosexual relationships altogether and simply stop relating to each other intimately. Instead, they turn for love and sexuality to those of their own sex.

Men and women alike have been victims of this socialization process that has caused them to fear and hate each other. While all seek attachment in ways that feel good and are satisfying, their gender defenses continually frustrate, disappoint and "trap" them without their knowledge.

Intimacy is impossible so long as men and women

reach out to each other to compensate for their own deficiencies and to be made whole. Nor is intimacy possible between two people who see each other as symbols and objects, and who see the partner as expecting and tolerating only certain appropriate responses based on his or her own needs. The misguided tendency to place the blame on specific issues rather than on the process, and the frustration that builds as a result, brings men and women inevitably to a highly cautious, hit-and-run way of relating, in order to avoid any contact that might suck them into an "intimacy" that inevitably turns love into hate.

3 Role, Ritual, and Religion: The Three R's of Traditional Relationships

ROLES ARE THE STRUCTURES that tell you how you should be and feel in a relationship. *Rituals* are the compulsive, predictable behaviors that fill the gaping spaces of an intrinsically empty relationship by structuring it with the specifics of what to do and when. *Religion* provides the rationalizing system that allows one to remove oneself from the here and now, while focusing instead on a "higher purpose." At the same time, it tends to create enormous pressure on couples to conform by telling them in unequivocal terms what "correct" or "spiritual" behavior and feelings are in a relationship. Thus, those who are in touch with their feelings of unhappiness and frustration often end up living two lives, the one they present to their religious peer community and the one they experience inside themselves and live out at home.

While the three r's of role, ritual, and religion seem on the surface to be the forces that sustain the man-woman relationship and the traditional family, actually they disguise its fundamental emptiness and the tension, anger, and resistance that inevitably build up in it.

These same three processes, which at first bind the traditional couple together, also make the long-term relationship psychologically expensive and a painful disillusionment. Each, upon psychological examination, is seen to have as its underpinning the word "should." "Should," in turn, is often motivated by guilt, which creates underlying resentment over feel'ng pressured and intimidated. Also, this leads to feelings of self-hatred when the three r's are not fulfilled in the way they are "supposed" to be. This is the inevitable end point of a relationship that was bolstered by the external pressure of the three r's and the absence of an equal focus on internal experience.

Relationships obviously don't last as long today as they used to in the days of our grandparents. This is often explained negatively. We are told that we have become too selfish or narcissistic. This is blamed as the *cause* rather than being viewed as the *effect* of the breakdown of male-female relationships.

The happy relationship of the past is a nostalgic illusion and distortion, like "remembrances" of the joys of the simple country life, joys that few ever experienced.

A group of California researchers interviewed more than thirty-five couples who had been married for fifty years or more. "We were looking for couples who could share their wisdom. They couldn't. They were just as confused as young couples. What made them unhappy when they first got married made them unhappy 50 years later."

A researcher at California State University reported similar findings. "We would get so sad at the end of an interview that we couldn't do another for two days. . . . Then we would go up to the door of the next one with our tape recorders in hand, praying, 'I hope we get a happy one.' "

That a couple had lived together for fifty years was not an expression of happiness. Rather, one researcher reported that for these people the marriage, not happiness, was important. There was an attitude that "we survived the Depression. We survived our marriage. . . . They didn't believe in divorce. . . . It was not an option."[1]

These couples had worked out rules to avoid painful conflicts. They ignored conflicts rather than risk talking about them. They kept their feelings from one another. The examination and sharing of feelings was subordinated to keeping the peace, maintaining a front, and "making the marriage work."

The *should* that underlies each of the three r's causes us to feel guilty when we experience our resistances to conforming, and angry when we do things in contradiction to what we feel or want. Most of the time, the negative and resistant feelings are blocked and repressed. In their place symptoms appear, such as the housewife's sundry illnesses and lethargy or the husband's drinking, irritability, preoccupation, and detachment when he is at home. In the meantime, we may blame and resent our partners for "making us unhappy," or seek escape and relief in distraction and emotional distance until the dam finally breaks and a flood of rage pours through, causing dissolution of the relationship or severe trauma. It is at this time that we experience all our repressed resistances and emotions directly, and our once loved partner becomes transformed into a source of antagonism and revulsion.

ROLES: BEING WHAT WE'RE SUPPOSED TO BE AND FEELING WHAT WE'RE SUPPOSED TO FEEL

The prescribed roles of intimate life—husband, wife, father, mother, lover, and so forth—carry with them implicit, powerful, and rigid mandates that inevitably produce painful conflict in every aware person, simply because role demands are rigid and specific whereas inner feelings and responses are constantly changing. Only a repressed and mechanical person, out of touch with his feelings, can feel and be what he is "supposed" to feel and be. *The inner sense of being abnormal, different, bad, hostile, disturbed, or whatever is therefore the inevitable inner experience of any person trying to live up to rigid role dictates.*

Wives are supposed to love their husbands; husbands are supposed to sexually desire their wives a certain number of times a week; neither are supposed to experience boredom with each other, or resistance to performing their functions—having children, keeping house, preparing meals, eating and sleeping together, coming home each day, and so on. When a husband finds himself not wanting to come home after work, when a wife finds herself not wanting to perform certain, domestic chores, when either one sexually desires others, guilt ensues and role defensiveness promotes the repression and denial of these feelings.

To escape from the discomfort of the conflict

between what they feel and what they're supposed
to feel, partners use socially approved ways to create
distance between themselves. One of the most
common of these in our society is television.

One hundred and eighty-four habitual television
viewers were asked to renounce the tube for a year.
They were paid for every day of self-denial. At first
they seemed to be happy to be free of it. They went
to the movies more often, visited relatives, and read
books.

Though they received payment for their "self-
denial," none held out for more than five months.
What drove them back to the television was the
increased tension at home, in bed, and at work.
Spouse violence and disciplining of the children by
hitting increased. With the television on again,
aggression decreased and sexual habits went back to
normal.[2]

A parallel revelation occurred after a recent
nationwide television-actors' strike, which stripped
television of most of its first-run programming. The
Nielsen television ratings showed that the strike,
which produced a prime-time schedule dominated
by reruns, had virtually no impact on viewing levels.
In fact, the figures for the entire seven-week period
of the strike even showed a sliver of an increase in
the number of households with their sets on. The
conclusion drawn was that American televison
viewers will watch *anything*. It was conjectured
that a half-hour program of television color bars
could end up at the top of the ratings.[3]

Feeling oneself to be crazy within the structure of
a traditional relationship would therefore seem to
be a normal response. This inner sense of something
being wrong or abnormal is an ackowledgment of

the important truth that in the process of trying to be "normal," our role-dictated behavior is splitting us off from our inner experience, annihilating the real self.

When role structure breaks down, its tenuous nature is exposed and the relationship may disintegrate entirely. Such was frequently the case in the last two decades, when many women overtly resisted and refused to play their expected roles.

One woman recounted her experience of going from housewife to working person thus:

In the spring of 1970, Alan was laid off from his aerospace job. Prior to this, I had proposed getting a job many times, always to be told that I mustn't do so, at least until our youngest was in school. Now, as weeks went by with no luck in job hunting, I persuaded him that it was time for me to go to work.

I took a job on the night shift of a large data-processing company, as a credit clerk. This was done so I could be at home during the day while my husband looked for work. During this family crisis, I had every intention of selflessly sharing the financial burdens. I saw myself as a heroine, a strong helpmate doing her part in time of trouble.

But that wasn't the way it worked out. Indeed, though I didn't realize it at first, the day I was hired was the beginning of the last chapter in our marriage. Free at last from my surburban cage, I became somebody I didn't recognize. The next few months were not dull. Indeed, it seemed that the entire office was a stage—set, lighted, peopled by actors, and just waiting for my triumphant entrance.

I quickly fell in love with one married man, who gave me quite a romantic whirl. When that finally ended, another stepped forward to take his place. Following that brief but intensely physical affair another man entered my life (he was later to become my present husband).

Meanwhile, back at home, things went from bad to worse. I was riding an emotional roller coaster I couldn't get off (and didn't want to).

I was free at last—living the kind of exciting life I knew I was meant for.

I stopped going to the ritual Sunday dinners at my in-laws' house. I enrolled in college as a freshman.

My husband started getting up whenever I got home from work, even though he surely needed his sleep. I took these late-night opportunities to tell him that our marriage was over. I laid on him all the frustrations I had felt during the eleven years we had been married, and accused him of treating me badly even before our marriage. I told him he thought only of himself and had never really loved me. I said that now I had friends, and lovers too, who really appreciated me. I told him I wanted out—out of our dull, boring, loveless marriage!

He tried at first to be reasonable—to talk sense to me—but I wasn't listening. He got angry and said, "You're digging your grave with your cunt!" (Strong words for him and quite out of character.) He pleaded with me. Finally, he wept.

Nothing worked. I was much too far beyond caring to be reached. I moved out.

Women's and men's liberation is resisted and experienced as a threat because of an underlying sense that without the traditional role structure there might be little or no basis for an ongoing relationship. Those who resist the loosening-up of men's and women's roles most vociferously probably fear this the most. For indeed, traditional relationships often have little that feels good in the here and now, little that would draw and keep the couple together for the spontaneous pleasure of each other's company if they didn't have to be together. Consequently, when the role structure begins to crumble, so does the relationship.

Those who advocate a return to traditional role playing are chasing an illusion. Traditional role playing only disguises the reduction of its participants to the destructive level of the machine and the child, eternally in conflict.

While there are those who would rationalize that clearly defined role structures are necessary for the survival of society, when role behavior engulfs personal identity, inner feelings are inevitably repressed and make both partners victims of themselves and the relationship, as the seepage of repressed resentment continually contaminates the interaction. Most who survive it are left disillusioned and even embittered. As life becomes more predictable and joyless, even their children, for whom they believe they did it all, end up resenting them.

RITUALS: THE TIES THAT BIND

A personal shorthand equation of mine is "The bigger the diamond engagement ring, the emptier the relationship." Put another way, the more traditional the relationship, the emptier the interaction between the man and the woman, and the more it requires rituals to fill it up. It begins during courtship, when they dress up to go out and eat, with him driving, her being "nice," him paying the check, her making him look good, and so on. Later there may be meals at specific appointed times, the good-night kiss, an attachment to certain television series, Saturday morning grocery shopping, Sunday church services, or daily jogging.

A ritual is any "have-to" behavior that is predictably and compulsively engaged in. Personal feelings are secondary to these mandates. You give the birthday gift or celebrate Mother's Day whether you feel like it or not.

Transgressing a ritual usually causes discomfort or hostility. For example, a husband gets angry when dinner is late or if his wife doesn't want sex on a given night of the week when they usually have it. Or the wife gets angry because her husband forgot to kiss her at the door or does not wish to visit his in-laws on Sunday afternoon. Often there is an enraged outburst. *The one who did not carry out the ritual is made to feel guilty while the "denied" person feels rejected and angry.*

Rituals disguise the process of the relationship, what it would look like if left to spontaneous interaction. Rituals also act as a bullying force. You feel compelled by them. The resistance and resentment surrounding a ritualistic "should" response emerges indirectly. A woman, for example, who is having sex because she "should," may readily become irritable and upset at the first little thing that goes wrong. A man who comes home for dinner at six, though he would have preferred being elsewhere, may show resentment through detachment, distraction, forgetting things, the nonparticipation in the conversation at the table, or may suddenly explode over a minor incident.

Premarital jitters, postpartum blues, stuffing oneself to discomfort at Thanksgiving, depression at Christmas, or an angry outburst during an anniversary celebration may all be manifestations of the repressed resistance that lies behind rituals. They are performed automatically to prevent guilt, rather than as a joyous, genuinely motivated expression of good feelings in the relationship.

In my research on people's honeymoon experiences, a large percentage of those looking back years later expressed disappointment, particularly women, who felt freer to be honest about their feelings. Having sex, doing things together, and "being nice" to each other are all a part of the rituals or supposed-tos of honeymoons. There is great pressure to suppress any resistances, boredom, or conflicting feelings. Consequently, it is not uncommon for one partner or both to drink too much or become ill during the honeymoon, shortening the length of the trip. The honeymoon experience is saturated with ritualistic behavior and expectations that produce sudden, unpredictable outbursts of anger over petty incidents, such as "You left a dirty washcloth in the tub." "You didn't hold my hand during the movie." "Why did you talk to that man (or woman) so long?" "You could have asked me what wine I wanted before you ordered."

Rituals fit the pattern described by Parkinson's Law: "Work expands so as to fill the time available for its completion. . . . The thing to be done swells in importance and complexity in a direct ratio with the time to be spent."[4]

It was formerly believed, for example, that household appliances would greatly reduce the amount of time and effort spent doing chores. However, there is no end to compulsive attention to detail *when chores are the rituals needed to keep things predictable, structured, and controlled.*

Researchers Walter R. Nord and Robert Costigan of Washington University studied the effect of a four-day work week on employee's lives. The study was conducted using one hundred employees at a pharmaceutical company in St. Louis. Approximately two thirds of those responding to a questionnaire after six and thirteen weeks reported that the new schedule had a favorable effect on their home lives. *But after one year only 45 percent felt that way.*[5]

Applied to traditional relationships, the principle is that rituals are needed to avoid spontaneous encounters and empty spaces in time, and will, therefore, continually expand to consume all available time.

Even sports and games become rigid rituals when they are used to fill unconsciously feared free time. Jogging or playing golf on a prescribed, regular basis are examples. Joggers are known to become irritable when they can't jog. This phenomenon is often rationalized by physiological explanations, rather than being recognized as the seepage of repressed anger that is being contained by compulsive behavior.

In general, the more polarized the couple in their masculine-feminine conditioning, the less they can share on an active, daily basis. Consequently, they require a maximum of ritualistic behavior to structure the relationship. Contrariwise, the more two people choose each other as partners out of genuine liking rather than ability to play a role, the less ritualized their interaction will need to be.

It's not in the *what*, but in the *how* that rituals can be recognized. A good-night kiss can be joyfully and passionately given. However, it becomes a ritual if no real choice is being made. If you don't do it you feel guilty, and if you do it you may experience traces of resentment over feeling coerced.

RELIGION: THE CONTROL AND SANCTIONING OF MARITAL UNHAPPINESS

When relationships don't feel good and begin to fall apart, religion is frequently used in an attempt to bind them together. Religion sanctions the traditional structures of marriage and family; encourages the denial of conflict, resistance, and anger; and provides an external focus to distract one from relationship discontent. For example, the Bible states that husbands and wives are to become one (Genesis 2:24), God builds the family (Psalm 127), and husbands are to love their wives (Colossians 3:19). In effect, this takes the pressure off the couple by allowing both to separate themselves from their real feelings, turning the fate of the relationship over to a divine power and utilizing the standards it sets forth.

In her book *Mine Eyes Have Seen the Glory*, Anita Bryant, staunch religionist, indicates that she did not want to marry her former husband, Bob Green. Reflecting the biblical teaching that wives should submit to their husbands, she wrote of how she suppressed her resistant, angry feelings toward her husband, who had begun to control her life on every level. "That's how good a manager my husband is. He willingly handles all the business in my life—even to including the Lord's business. Despite our sometimes violent scraps, I love him for it."[6]

Later, she wrote, "Only as I practice yielding to Jesus can I learn to submit, as the Bible instructs me, to the loving leadership of my husband,"[7] and only after ending the relationship with her husband was she finally able to express the full extent of her rage toward him for controlling her and destroying much of her career by pressing her to become a militant crusader against homosexuality.

Marabel Morgan, religion-oriented spokesperson for traditional female behavior in marriage and author of the bestselling *Total Woman*, designed to teach women how to please their husbands, described her painful marriage before discovering God's will: "I was helpless and unhappy."[8]

Morgan wrote *The Total Woman*, she said, after six years of marriage, when things were really beginning to fall apart. "I had never seen a happy marriage. My mother was married three times while I was growing up."[9]

After a marriage with four children, which brought her to the point of total desperation, Ruth Carter Stapleton, sister of Jimmy Carter, surrendered to Jesus.[10] In her book *The Gift of Inner Healing*, Stapleton gives this counsel to a young, unhappily married woman: "Try to spend a little time each day visualizing Jesus coming in the door from work. Then see yourself walking up to him, embracing him. Say to Jesus, 'It's good to have you come home, Nick.' "[11]

Lois Robertson, seventeen years old and a virgin at the time of her marriage, raised in Kentucky, remembers that her husband was gone for a month on a business trip shortly after their wedding.

> Funny, I thought I should miss him more! I didn't! I was at home just as if I weren't married at all.

Sundays I went to church just as I always had done. I found a scripture in I Peter 3:2 that said I should have reverence for my husband.

I spent all Sunday afternoon picturing myself doing that, and thought we would have a fine marriage because I would learn to cook and take care of the house and be just the kind of wife God wanted me to be. I felt good thinking and planning for the future.

I was bored so I got a job working at the nearby supermarket. I liked being around other people and talking and laughing with the customers, but my husband didn't want me to work there. He said the men who came in were too rough and he thought I was flirting. We had our first fight and I threw a glass across the kitchen and broke it. He grabbed me and threw me over his knee and whacked me and said I was acting like a spoiled brat. Later we made up. He took me on a vacation and I quit my job.

I really was bored staying home. I cleaned the house, planted flowers in the yard, learned to fix special recipes, and read novels.

I thought sex was pretty much overrated, though my husband thought it was the only thing. After I had a baby, which hurt more than having both legs cut off, I was so scared of sex that it got to be a real burden. Then I found my husband had his first affair with a waitress he met while traveling.

I felt the worst I had ever felt in my life when I found out about it. I cried, then I became enraged and threw temper tantrums.

I got some books and magazines from the library and thought I would just escape for a while. One of the books I read was called *Christian Sex Ethics* by V. A. Demant. It said certain things I tried to live up to. "In the love relation of men and women there is more than primarily the need for sex but the need for another person . . . be forgiving one to another even as Christ has forgiven you."

Still I had trouble trusting my husband. I kept watching and wondering whenever he was late if he was "messing around" again. I began to be attracted to other men. But the Bible verse from I Corinthians which advises to "flee fornication [for] he that committeth fornication sins against his own body" kept going through my mind. In the book *Christian Sex Ethics*, I had read that adultery was both a social and moral offense.

I became very moody and withdrawn. When I cried, my husband would get even madder at me and sometimes leave the apartment in a huff. I started going to church two to three times a week feeling very sanctimonious and superior and virtuous about myself.

He began insisting that I bake my own bread, that I stay at home and cook everything from scratch, that I sew shirts for him, and that the ironing be done perfectly, and he did not want me to have women friends come to my home to visit me. He even started to read the bible himself to quote to me from I Peter 3:6: ". . . Sara obeyed Abraham, calling him lord. . . ."

I went back to school, got a degree and started working as a teacher. Things got worse until the marriage finally collapsed. Perhaps it would have survived if my husband had accepted the Bible teaching of I Peter 3:7 to give "honour unto the wife," and also Ephesians 5:25: "Husbands, love your wives, even as Christ also loved the Church and gave himself for it. . . ."

In all these instances, religion served the function of diverting anger, resistance, boredom, sexual impulses, and other "forbidden" or seemingly unmanageable feelings. These inner experiences were seen as obstacles to overcome rather than guideposts bringing one closer to oneself and the reality of the relationship. In general, the specific form of the religious activity, be it meditation, a quasimystical cult experience, or a traditional religious one, is irrelevant so long as it fulfills the function of removing the emotions of the moment and the genuine experience of the relationship, while providing "answers" and "solutions" to its problems.

I believe that the more traditional the relationship, the greater the degree of conflict and repressed as well as overt anger, and, therefore, the greater the attraction to and utilization of religious practices and teachings.

Also it is my impression that the experience of religious conversion in times of marital turmoil most often comes first to the woman, who then brings her husband along into it. From the perspective of masculine and feminine defenses, religion fits the latter best, because by encouraging harmony, patience, and understanding, it reinforces women's repression of aggression and their tendency to withdraw from conflict. By encouraging obedience and submission to God (and husband), it reinforces dependency and the repression of assertion. By making fornication sinful, it reinforces the tendency toward sexual repression. Therefore, women are more comfortable in taking on a religious consciousness.

In comparison, men in these relationships generally come off second best and looking like hardened sinners, the reason being that the assumption of a religious orientation and masculine conditioning are a poor match. Masculine defenses produce an exaggerated sense of self-importance, an aggressive tendency, sexual obsession, and resistance to being submissive. All are antithetical to devout, conflict-free religiosity.

While it fits her psychological "nature" or defense structure, and also provides her with a natural instrument of power over her husband (who will constantly be struggling with religion and falling short), it also blocks her growth. Rather than teaching her to fight it out, assert her needs, grow toward autonomy, and become comfortable with overt sexuality, religion encourages the continued repression of all of these.

All recent exploration of the life of famed literary figure Max Perkins, nurturer of some of America's great authors, including Ernest Hemingway, F. Scott Fitzgerald, and Thomas Wolfe, discussed Perkins's relationship with his wife, Louise, a woman with "talent galore for a career on the stage. Her husband, Max, however, extracted a promise from her before they were married that she would not become a professional actress. He was rigid in blocking her aspirations and pleadings for her own career as an actress. They fought bitterly for years until, eventually, Louise converted to Catholicism, much to Max's disgust, and laid her histrionic talent on the altar of Jesus Christ with a fervor that came to seem like madness. Not satisfied with going to mass every day and cloistering herself on week-long retreats, she sprinkled holy water all over the house, dousing Max's pillow several times a week."[12]

A man is caught in a double-bind. If he fits the image of the ideal male, he falls short of the sanctified religious values. He will be left feeling guilty and wanting, accusing himself of being a religious hypocrite. If he does not fulfill the masculine ideal while managing to live up to the religious one, he will feel self-hating and inadequate for not being manly enough.

The short-run support provided by religion, like the other two r's, is paid for by sacrificing the growth of each partner toward a healthy, totally aware sense of interpersonal reality, and the development of tools to deal effectively with the problems that arise. The three r's do not create the problems of a relationship. They merely are used to disguise them and to prevent their conscious, authentic resolution. Healthy relationships are free of the rigid use of the three r's. They are based on two people who strive to know each other and deal with each other transparently and directly in the here and now.

4 Sex at Cross-purposes:
A Cruel Paradox

IN RECENT YEARS the prevalence of "sexual symptoms" has climbed steadily and caused the Masters and Johnson Institute to write in its newsletter that "most professionals in the sex field are convinced that there is a very high incidence of sexual difficulty among couples who see themselves as normal and who do not seek therapy of any kind."[1]

A study recently published in the *New England Journal of Medicine* arrived at a similar conclusion. It analyzed the responses of one hundred "happily married" couples. Forty percent of the men reported "erectile or ejaculatory dysfunction," while 63 percent of the women reported "arousal or orgasmic dysfunction." In addition, 50 percent of the men and 77 percent of the women reported difficulties that were not strictly speaking dysfunctional in nature, but included lack of interest or inability to relax.[2]

However, it is a mistake when partners in relationships are persuaded by the experts to concentrate on a problem called sexual dysfunction. In reality, when we examine the psychological underpinnings of the traditional relationship, it becomes clear that sexual disappointment, feelings of inadequacy, and other difficulties are built-in parts of everybody's experience.

Indeed, it is in the sexual arena that the mismatching of the sexes, a phenomenon I have termed sex at cross-purposes, caused by the polarization of masculine and feminine conditioning, can be most clearly seen. Ironically, the more perfectly romantic the match in the traditional sense (e.g., football hero and cheerleader), the more powerfully they will experience the impact and agony of sexual pitfalls, of the gap between what they expect and what actually occurs.

For the man, sex traditionally has been the primary proving ground for his masculinity. The goal of masculine conditioning is a machinelike state in which he strives to be a perfect performer, and his sexuality is a powerful manifestation of this dehumanization.

He relates to his penis as if it were a piece of plumbing or mechanical equipment. It either "works" or "doesn't work." If it doesn't work, he feels an intense urgency to "get it fixed" as fast as possible, just as if it were some malfunctioning piece of machinery.

Furthermore, if it doesn't work, he disowns responsibility. "I really want to—there must be something wrong with it," he thinks. He has an adversary relationship with his penis; he feels victimized by this capricious organ between his legs that seems to have a mind of its own. His feelings of failure, self-hatred, fear, and inadequacy drive him to regain his performance competence as quickly as possible when a problem arises. At the suggestion that his sexual problem and "malfunctioning" penis may be reflecting meaningful and important feelings about the quality of his relationship, or his distorted masculine expectations, he becomes impatient, threatened, and resentful.

Paradoxically, traditional masculine defenses inevitably create the very blocks and impasse points that preclude a man's being the great lover he imagines and wishes himself to be. Specifically, masculinity has produced his need to control, his goal orientation, his impatience with and lack of sensitivity to emotions, his compulsion to prove himself, his inability to talk about areas of anxiety and sexual ignorance, and his failure to honestly acknowledge his lack of desire or to confront and resolve sexual conflicts and turn-offs in his relationships. Ultimately he will be defeated by his tendency to attach himself to a woman whom he places on a pedestal as a chaste madonna, and who will cling and threaten him with an extreme "intimacy" need that will greatly diminish his sexual motivation and ability to perform.

He, of course, is only half the problem. As a young girl, a female has sexuality largely repressed. She learns that sex is something that men want and "good girls" don't "give" or really need. Later, sex becomes something she can barter for "love." Sex may be enjoyed under special conditions of "commitment" and "intimacy," but at the same time, she feels she can do without it if the circumstances are not exactly right.

Because of the essentially childlike nature of femininity, she lacks the assertiveness to define and initiate what she wants sexually, and the aggression to fight out and resolve a conflict when it arises, as it surely must. Instead, she perceives herself as vulnerable to sexual victimization and exploitation, like a helpless infant, and therefore builds up a defensive attitude.

Her repressed sexual drive means that it is hard for her to know when, in fact, she really desires sex. Instead, she misunderstands and tends to be repulsed by what seems in her eyes to be the man's indiscriminate sexual appetite. She comes to perceive him as a predator because he pursues sexual pleasure casually, outside the bounds of intimacy.

The man reinforces her immature quality. He wants to believe in her innocence, in the specialness of her sexual feelings toward him, and in her naïveté. He would even like to think that he taught her everything she knows.

Likewise, she reinforces his machinelike consciousness. When she falls in love, she sees in him qualities of strength and ability to perform that he does not really have—and that puts great pressure on him. She expects him to be a self-confident take-charge lover and to be always ready, as part of her infantile perception of him as a superman, just as he expects all this of himself. She also sees him as having this capacity as part of his masculine "magic" rather than as part of a mutual stimulation pattern. Her intense "love," therefore, becomes a threat, as he falls into feeling he must perform whenever she is loving or turned on. In fact, the reverse is likely to happen. The closer and the more "loving" (attached to and dependent on him) she gets, the more his sexual response will wither. Her childlike belief that his sexuality is linked to his lovingness is then affected, and she takes his lack of erection or urgent response as a personal rejection. Also, her perception of him as infinitely powerful is shattered. He, in turn, is flooded with feelings of failure.

In general, masculine and feminine conditioning makes men and women a mismatch in bed. Their polarization causes them to be ill suited for, and ultimately enemies of, each other sexually.

SEX AT CROSS-PURPOSES: THE MANY MISMATCHES

The Conquest-Intimacy Mismatch

Masculine conditioning results in sex being perceived in the context of challenge and lust. Feminine conditioning produces a perception of sex in the context of love and intimacy.

As a young boy, a male learns that sex is a challenge created by the resistant woman, one that he must overcome because she does not really want it. Because his intimate capacities are largely extinguished, sex is lust—looking at and feeling women's breasts and genitals.

Traditionally, as a young girl, a female learns that sex is only permissible when linked with love, commitment, and intimacy. Sex means loving and being close. She tends to be threatened by and uncomfortable with a man's urgent and seemingly impersonal approach, while he is threatened by her demand that commitment and emotional intimacy accompany sexual activity.

Consequently, he will tend to be turned on most when she is turned on least, and vice versa. That is, he is aroused most by challenge and emotional distance—the early encounters when sex is new and different, when the woman is more a fantasy than a person and is resistant, unavailable, and uncomfortable because of the lack of intimacy and commitment. Assuming the relationship continues and she gets from him the commitment she wants, she may then attempt to free herself up sexually. As she does that, the challenge-and-conquest factor diminishes for him, and the demands for closeness increase, and his sex drive and the quality of his "performance" wane.

In those instances where the very traditional woman never gives up her perception of sex as a duty or gift to her husband, he may continue to remain aroused because the challenge is always present. However, because she never *really* wants sex, she is left feeling used and insensitively treated throughout the marriage, and the resentment accumulates. Eventually, she may use illness or other excuses to withdraw from sex.

The Sensuality-Sexuality Mismatch

She is conditioned to be sensual and not sexual, whereas he is conditioned to be sexual and not sensual.

As a young girl, she is kissed, held, cuddled, and stroked, and learns to be comfortable expressing herself that way. At the same time she learns that explicit sexuality is dirty and threatening.

For a young boy, kissing, cuddling, hugging, and stroking are sissy behavior. However, sex and being able to get a girl to supply it are considered a validation of masculinity.

Therefore, while making love, she will be prone to say, "Why can't we hold each other more—be next to each other? You hardly even touch me. Why does it always have to mean sex right away when we get close? Sometimes I just want to lie next to you without doing anything."

He, on the other hand, is prone to say, if he is honest and open about it, "You never *really* want to have sex. All you want to do is hold and hug. How long do we have to do that until you're ready to have sex?"

She may pretend to experience orgasm and sexual excitement to please him, when basically all she wants is closeness. He may pretend pleasure in being close when all he really wants is sexual release.

Resentment will build on both sides. He will feel impatient, pressed, and bored by her seemingly insatiable need for closeness. She will feel exploited and unloved as a result of his direct and seemingly impersonal approach to sex.

The Emotional-Intellectual Mismatch

Because her focus is on feeling, she will want to deepen the relationship emotionally. She is uncomfortable and impatient with his preoccupation with positions, techniques, statistics, and fantasy games. On the other hand, his emphasis is more on the how-to, the mechanics of performance. He is uncomfortable and impatient with her emphasis on sharing feelings and being intimate.

Their conditioning also produces mismatched communication. It prevents them from really understanding each other's distress and fulfilling each other's needs.

The "Fragile Male Ego"—"Sensitive Madonna" Mismatch

He tends to respond protectively and to withhold information he thinks will hurt his wife's or lover's feelings, and might cause her to withdraw in retaliation.

She learns that his masculine ego is fragile in sexual matters and that she must make him feel good about himself as a man. Also, she wants to avoid confrontation, negative interchanges, or encounters that are "unkind." Therefore when she is unhappy about sexual matters between them, she tends to hide these feelings.

Consequently, there is a careful, walking-on-eggshells relationship between them, rather than honest communication, assertiveness, and confrontation.

The "Goal Oriented"—"Process Oriented" Mismatch

He is goal oriented. For him, sex has a beginning, a middle, and an end point. It is difficult for him to transcend the concept of a logical progression in sex, with the first kiss leading to intercourse.

She is process oriented. Her motivation and pleasure come from the experience of being close. She resents his quick, predictable progression. To her, his goal orientation is the epitome of being unromantic.

With her diffuse romantic orientation and need for reassurance, she seems to him oblivious that time exists at all. Her romantic expectations make him self-conscious and tense, and he sees her as making unending demands for closeness.

The Actor-Reactor Mismatch

His conditioning teaches him to be the initiator, the director, the actor. Femininity trains her to take her cues from him and to be naïve—the reactor.

Because he is the actor, he feels responsible and guilty when the sex is unsatisfactory. Underneath his guilt, he also accumulates resentment over always having to read her mind, to decipher when and how she likes it.

As a reactor, she comes to feel resentful over being controlled and used. Sex becomes another accommodation to him, something that she feels she engages in according to his needs. She comes to feel rage over this.

In extreme cases, as the reactor she feels dirty, used, and even raped by his control. As the actor he feels manipulated by the way she seems to dangle her sexuality as a prize, and even when she gives it he feels he has been done a favor, because true passion is missing.

Linked to this actor-reactor mismatch is the impossible bind actors and reactors put each other in. If he is the initiator, she comes to feel controlled. If he doesn't initiate sex, he seems unmanly in her eyes and very possibly nothing will happen between them, because she won't fill the vacuum by assuming the role of actor. If she doesn't initiate sex, he complains that he doesn't know what she wants or when she wants it. If she does initiate things, however, he feels pressured to perform and sees her as aggressive and unfeminine.

This actor-reactor phenomenon blocks growth and change because his role as an actor means that he must be the sexual expert and teacher, while she is the reacting student. He is, therefore, fearful of acknowledging ignorance lest he seem unmanly, and she is fearful of seeming too knowledgeable by making suggestions that might insult his masculinity and cause her to seem unfeminine.

The Animal-Madonna Mismatch

For the traditional man, sex is a major obsession. Indeed, for many men it is the most important aspect of their lives. A typical husband quoted in a study of the marital relations of blue-collar workers stated it cogently: "Sex is the most important thing, say 95% of marriage."[3]

For traditional women, sex is not a primary, conscious preoccupation in a relationship. Some women barely tolerate it, as a wife in this same study of blue-collar marriages stated: "He thinks sex is very important. He couldn't live without it, I guess. . . . Me, I could do without it; our feelings are completely opposite."[4]

She cannot understand and resents his sexual preoccupation, which she sees as animalistic. He cannot understand and resents her seeming lack of a sex drive. This probably intensifies his sexual preoccupation, just as his obsessive interest in sex exaggerates her defensiveness and absence of desire.

The Sexist Symbols Mismatch

She uses sexuality partially as a defense to compensate for inner feelings of helplessness and powerlessness. It gives her a source of power and control. He uses sexuality as a primary vehicle to prove that he is a man.

Every such sexual encounter will be depersonalized by the fact that she preceives men as sexually exciting on the basis of their power symbols, because she overcomes feelings of helplessness indirectly and defensively through them. He judges women as attractive based on their having physical features such as large breasts and a shapely figure, which validate him as a man in public. In that sense, both are unconsciously conditioned to be sexists. That is, their sexual attraction is not really based on the partner as a person, but on sexual symbols that validate each through the other.

While the initial attraction may be powerful, the underlying sense of being used as an object by the other person will eventually produce resentment on both sides. He will distrust her pronouncements of love and come to feel she only cares because of his role as a provider. Meanwhile, she will feel resentful over being seen as a sex object and will doubt his love for her.

The Monogamy-Freedom Mismatch

Initially she wants a monogamous, committed relationship, while he wants freedom. He fears she will manipulate him into a permanent relationship, and she fears he will exploit her sexually and then abandon her.

These opposing attitudes suggest that he will be sexually restless in a monogamous relationship, fantasizing about other women, while she will be unhappy in any sustained sexual involvement that does not become a committed, exclusive relationship.

Whether men or women are basically monogamous or not is not a relevant question, because their behaviors are distortions produced by their masculine and feminine conditioning. That is, the woman's desire for permanent, exclusive attachment stems from conditioning to feel guilt over sexuality that is not sanctioned by an intimate, committed bond, while also creating in her a deeply rooted sense of vulnerability and helplessness because of the repression of aggressive or autonomous behavior. She is therefore prone to seek permanent attachment to a man who will take primary responsibility for these areas. While the woman's monogamous orientation has been seen as a part of her special virtue, on a deeper level it simply reflects her defensive compensation.

The man's glorification of freedom is as false and defensive as is hers of attachment and monogamy. His early socialization taught him that dependency, loss of control, and emotional expressiveness are unmasculine. Also, he has been conditioned to find satisfaction in sex with challenge, emotional distance, and conquest. Therefore, his need to prove himself sexually will not be satisfied in a one-to-one commitment where there is permanence and closeness.

LACK OF DESIRE AS AN INCREASINGLY COMMON "SYMPTOM" IN MARRIAGE

Those couples that stay together may find their sexual involvement reduced to an abysmal level—a huge drop from their once lofty fantasies of ecstatic sex.

In their most recent book, William H. Masters and Virginia Johnson, who have gathered perhaps the greatest amount of specific information on traditional heterosexual couples, described these couples as generally being bumblers in their lovemaking.

They tend to misread signals, hurry sex, and communicate poorly.

According to Masters and Johnson, both men and women are woefully ignorant of each other's needs. Women are described as having no idea of how men like to be touched sexually, and the majority of men massage the women's genitals in an insensitive, off-putting manner. Furthermore, the obsession with reaching orgasm, on the part of both men and women, considerably impairs the experience.[5]

The Hite Report: A Nationwide Study of Female Sexuality explicates discontent and frustration in traditional sexual relationships from the women's perspective. Some of Shere Hite's conclusions, based on her study of a large number of women, are:

1. Intercourse is not enough for most women to reach orgasm.
2. Sexist norms have determined that women be regarded as slow to reach arousal, rather than that men be regarded as unskilled
3. More women than ever before are having homosexual experiences.
4. Women can masturbate to orgasm easily and regularly.[6]

Well-known sex therapist and researcher Dr. Helen Singer Kaplan devoted an entire book to a phenomenon she terms ISD (inhibited sexual desire).[7]

It has been reported that "lack of sexual desire" is the complaint of as much as 40% of the patients who come to therapy centers, and that there are increasing numbers of people with "an actual phobia" about sex. They not only avoid sex, but have an active dislike of it, even the *thought* of it. Some can't stand to be touched, and the prospect of sexual activity makes them break out in a sweat or causes them to become nauseated.[8]

An attempt has even been made to transform the growing phenomenon of lack of desire into something fashionable. One newspaper termed it asexual chic and reported that increasing numbers of well-known people are choosing to withdraw from the sexual arena entirely.[9]

From the man's perspective, one writer spoke of the new breed of men in the making. "They're doing their own thing all right, which is to do little or nothing for women. Passive resistance in the most literal sense."[10]

SEXUAL DYSFUNCTION AND SEXISM

In traditional relationships a good sex life is largely a fiction, because there is no person-to-person sex, but only gender-defensive-motivated sex. So-called sexual dysfunction is an inevitability because the woman feels she is being insensitively related to, and the man feels constantly compelled to prove himself. He cannot say no and she cannot say yes in a fullhearted way. She uses sexuality for security and reassurance, and once those aims are fulfilled she is without a sexual motive. He uses sex for control, validation of his manliness, and assurance that she is still his possession, and when those goals are reached he is without a sexual motive. She is a sex object while he is a security object. Both experience sexual excitement as a by-product of defensive motives.

In part, the prevalent expectation of a regular sex life is the logical extension of the never-ending defensive male compulsion to prove his masculinity, and

the unending feminine defensive need for reassurance and security. Unlike all other species' sexual
relationships, those of human beings have no boundaries and limits, and therefore easily become a controlling monster.

The tyranny of statistics, leading to the notion of
a regular, "normal" sex life defined by numbers,
was the final nail in the coffin of traditional sex.
The expectation of an unendingly exciting sex life,
day in and day out, when superimposed on defensive sexual motivation, is inhuman cruelty to the
psyches of men and women.

The language and orientation of traditional sex
therapy reinforces the sexist perception of the man
as a sexual machine and the woman as his child-
victim whom he treats insensitively. Further, it tends
to reinforce the illusion that there is a right way to
do it, and a way to fix any problem.

Words such as "impotence" and "premature
ejaculation" are sexist in that they perpetuate the
belief that there is a correct way for men to perform,
ignoring the fact that the man's sexual response is
an expression of who he is and is linked to his
feelings, true desires, and the quality of the relationship. The label of impotence in itself is insulting
and damaging in its anxiety-producing impact. Every woman knows that her sexual response is vari-
able according to how she is feeling toward the man
and the state of mind she is in. For a traditional
man, however, there is only one correct way to be,
sexually: erect and in control, no matter what he
feels. This attitude leads to the absurd phenomenon
of his feeling distressed when he can't perform even
with a woman by whom he is bored or repelled.

Likewise, labels for feminine dysfunctions such

as vaginismus and frigidity are often misleading in that they imply a disorder rather than being understood as a direct result of a woman's early conditioning and her negative perception of the male "animal." These labels may not be as damaging to the woman as men's labels are to the man because her femininity and self-image are not as directly linked to being a sexual performer. Still, to become a total sexual being she must recognize that her body too reflects her emotions, and that if she is continually frigid or "dry" with a man, it may be a clear reflection of her feelings.

The ultimate, horrific end point of macho sexual consciousness is beginning to emerge fully in our culture. Less than ten years ago, the Masters and Johnson findings and the conclusions of most professional sex therapists were that less than 10 percent of male sexual dysfunction was caused by physiological problems. While the treatments still tended to be mechanical, at least they were not surgical.

Today, urologists are "discovering" and telling men that a much higher percentage of so-called impotence problems are the result of physical diffculties. I believe that this conclusion is mainly an outgrowth of male impatience, resistance, and disbelief in the personal and emotional origins of "dysfunction," and the desperate urgency produced by masculine conditioning to perform and "feel like a man." As a result, there is an ever increasing use of a nightmarish armamentarium of treatments, including silicone implants that produce a permanent erection, the inflatable prosthesis, and bypass surgery or revascularization. The latter involves transplanting a healthy artery from the abdomen to the penis so that it can collect blood around the "diseased" natural artery, again under the assumption that that is the real cause of the problem.

Is the man allowing himself to be sexually repaired for his woman's sake or for that of his own threatened ego? He has been conditioned to believe he should function a certain way and a certain number of times a week. Is the "equipment' *really* faulty or are his repressed feelings getting in the way? The belief many men have is that it is their obligation to have an erection, that the woman expects it, and that she might abandon him or look elsewhere if he fails to perform as he should. All of these assumptions need to be seriously questioned for, in the light of feminine conditioning, it is unlikely that her primary concern is his ever ready erection. Most women complain of relationship and affectional frustrations with their men, rather than sexual ones. In fact, it is not hard to imagine that women might be secretly repulsed by, or at best feel sorry for, men's desperate urgency to perform at all costs.

Both men and women are equally victims of sexual conditioning that puts their sexual needs together at cross-purposes. Frustration, disappointment, even disgust and a phobic attitude are the logical end points of traditional masculine-feminine conditioning. Thus, the thing committed couples anticipate and wish for most—an exciting, adventurous, experimental, and growing sexual relationship, with hours spent in ecstatic enjoyment of each other—will continually and frustratingly elude them.

5 "We-think": The Whole Is Smaller Than the Sum of Its Parts

"WE-THINK" is the loss of separate identity within the grinding confines of the traditional relationship. It is a tragic psychological phenomenon that makes both partners far less than they are or might become as separate beings outside of it. Recognizing and working to avoid being transformed by the we-think phenomenon is a critical aspect of the new male-female relationship.

As far back as 1854, a book titled *Marriage: Its History, Character and Results; Its Sanctities and Its Profanities; Its Science and Its Facts* predicted that a society which divided people into "parties of two" would progress to the point where human isolation was complete and each person doomed to hermitage. Traditional marriage, according to this book, signaled the end of personal development for husbands and wives and cut them off from meaningful relationships with others. It described the social relationships of couples as "transient, fragmentary and spasmodic." Women in particular were said to have their development abruptly terminated in marriage, which made them unsuited for mother-hood.[1]

Physician William A. Alcott, who wrote a series of advice books for women, also in the mid-1800's, noted that one of the most discouraging family problems was that men did not talk to their wives. Many of his female patients, he wrote, were low on energy and suffering from indefinable and indescribable feelings of ennui, which, for want of a better name, were all called nervousness. These women, according to Dr. Alcott, sought comfort and relief in over-eating (preferably sweets), drinking large quanities of tea and coffee, and sniffing ammonia or cologne. He wondered that more of these women didn't go mad.[2]

The change that has taken place since that time is that many women have begun to experience directly the blocked emotions and impulses that lie at the root of their symptoms. Specifically, feminist and other women's literature of the past two decades has articulated an awareness of the poisonous effects of the traditional marital roles and interactions on women's health and growth. Repeatedly described is the annihilation of the women's identity, resulting from the chemistry of marital togetherness. Rather than emerging and maintaining herself as a person, she experiences herself as a shadow of her husband.

While the woman's experience has been described clearly and repeatedly because her consciousness of herself as a victim gives her permission to express pain and outrage, it is not acceptable for men to complain or express their agony. Therefore, the isolation, constriction, and destruction of self that men experience in marriage have not been given equal regard and articulation. For the man, however, the result of the we-think phenomenon in the marital relationship is progressive isolation and friendlessness; an excessive and often pathetic dependency on his wife; the loss of his capacity to be open and playful; an increasing obsession with money, security, and the future; and anxiety regarding his sexuality and the increasing loss of most of his capacities except for that of work.

WE-THINK AND WOMEN

Writer Colette Dowling has described the insidious, overpowering experience of losing her identity once she became attached to and began living with the man who was to become her husband. "Oddly, from that moment on, I had trouble working," she writes. "The capacity for being alone in my head, which had developed nicely during the four years of my actually living alone, vanished suddenly. . . . I also seemed to have picked up an obsessive quirk. I began reworking every page I wrote about ten times, morbidly preoccupied with syntax and form, as if someone critical were looking over my shoulder. All passion went, all play. . . . My mind seemed bounded by the flowered walls of the bedroom and by the string of photographs which hung there of the two of us laughing together in the sunshine of a visit to Fire Island. Romance had inured me to reality once more. I was safe. I was wrapped in my room as in a womb, and no fitful glances at empty bank statements would propel me beyond its confines and into the real world."[3]

While it is customary to blame the sexist domination of men for women's loss of identity in marriage, Dowling knew this was not the cause in her case. Her husband was encouraging her career. "He'd grown tired of supporting me and had begun to insist that I do something about it. . . . With the surfacing of his discontent, I discovered something quite shocking about myself. I *want* to be supported . . . what I want is a full-time emotional protection, a buffer between me and the world. . . . It's conflict that clipped my wings, not him. *He wants me to fly.* He also wants me off his back. . . . This give-and-take, this daily opening oneself to the potential ravages of human encounter, is what's involved in being an adult and you know something . . . I resent hell out of it."[4]

A thirty-year-old divorced woman, speaking for herself and for a number of women acquaintances, described the powerful effect of we-think on her life and marriage:

Being of "marriageable age" and filled with negative, empty feelings, I reached the logical conclusion that I needed a husband. Lo and behold—one day an attractive male walked by. What's more, he seemed to like me! . . . Some sort of trigger went off in my brain and I was literally driven to become part of this person. I don't want to slide too quickly over this concept of drivenness because it was to influence my life for a long time to come, and I have watched it happen to other females I know. My whole being, my whole existence became focused on this one effort—to unite with this male whom I had sighted on. Every other thought or commitment became secondary to this purpose.

I'm spending a lot of time on my orientation as a female because I think men need to understand where women are coming from—why they are so sweet in the beginning and why they become so disappointed and resentful when they find out they have been lied to. Females aren't devious witches who will do anything to sucker a guy into tying the knot, then let the fangs come out once the trap has sprung. For them, it's like being promised a wonderfully sweet treat for twenty years and if one is deserving and follows the rules, the glory will be immeasurable. Then when we take a big bite, it turns out to be very sour indeed, and we feel tricked.

I let him be in charge of everything—what we did, how we did it, etc. . . . I was always available and desirous of being with him in any way. One thing I've noticed with myself and also with my female friends is that the more driven we are to attach, the sweeter and more giving we come across. The drivenness and the aggressiveness show in the things we do in private or around our girlfriends, but never around the guy we have sighted on.

When I looked at him, I saw my dream—a real Prince Charming. Two months from the time we met, we were married. I really got into the cooking and cleaning and laundry thing, and he came right home from work to his "little lover." It was lovely. We had a baby, I made him lovely hot lunches, we had another baby, I learned to sew and to make my own pickles.

But I was getting heavier somehow, and he was starting to bend under the load. The parts of me that I had been denying began to gradually sneak out. Little voices began popping up in the back of my brain. They weren't saying things like "Rita, you goofed it. You guys didn't know yourselves and each other before you got into this." Instead, they said, "He's not enough. He's not as smart as I thought. He's really klutzy. He's never going to go anywhere."

Ironically, it seems not to be that women are yelling first and loudest because they hurt more, but rather that they hurt less. While it would seem at first glance that women must be in worse shape if they are the first to yell, that does not follow when we consider that the need for survival requires adaptation. The more one is lost or buried or hurting, the less one will be able to cry out or to see because he will have had to accept more in order to survive.

Still another woman writer described the we-think process and its impact on her (italics added):

I remember, when Andy and I first met, how romantic and mystical it seemed that we could understand each other so perfectly. . . . We anticipated each other's statements.

After we were married, this magical sense that our souls were bound together was not enough to pull us through . . . *our romantic illusions propelled us into a fusion that brought out the worst in both of us.* We were becoming mirror-images, like the survivors of multiple anniversaries who can no longer differentiate where one's life leaves off and the other's begins.

We each gave up something to merge with each other. When we realized that this surrender was irreversible, we began to remember how very valuable our separate natures had been. It was only when we made the decision to separate that we started to recover a sense of personal identity and to understand that habit and financial arrangements had long outlived love. . . .

When we were living together, we had regrettably few meaningful relationships with "outsiders" and we smothered each other in the totality of "us," putting impossible demands on the marriage.[5]

Natalie Rogers, the daughter of Dr. Carl Rogers, one of America's most respected humanistic psychologists, did not escape the enormous impact of we-think in her marriage. Later, divorced, she reflected on her marital experience:

After being a very independent woman as a college student, it was just really astonishing what I did to myself, and what my husband colluded in when we got married. . . .

I really lost my sense of self. I disappeared to myself. To outsiders I looked happy and put-together—we were, you know, the handsome couple doing exciting things. But I was like a shell.

That's why I fear getting married again. Maybe it doesn't have to, but legalizing it seems to do that to women. The big fear is losing my identity again. Would I immediately begin to feel that I had to serve or accommodate? Would I have to give up being able to live at my own rhythm and pace? Would I have to give up some of the choices that I have now?

My divorce was the only thing I could do to save myself. It took a long time, and it was a very, very painful decision. It went against everything I believed in and wanted. But it was a matter of psychic survival to make the decision. And I must say that ever since I got divorced, I have really flourished.[6]

It undoubtedly seems to many men like a bewildering and enraging paradox that women press so hard for commitment and marriage, often against the man's resistance, only to later break away with such revulsion—often even when he apparently has done nothing more than fulfill his expected role. No irresponsibility, no violence, no bad habits, and yet he is still found wanting. Before marriage, his resistance to permanence and exclusivity was explained to him as fear of intimacy, and a sign of immaturity. Once in the marriage, he is blamed for having shackled the woman and blocked her growth and autonomy.

One woman reminisced about her rearing as a young girl, which clearly set the stage for the we-think phenomenon:

I was raised in a very strict way which taught me to be lady-like! Grandma taught me to sit with my skirts properly arranged over my knees. She taught me that girls do not climb trees, spit, swear (like my brothers were allowed to do). I quickly caught on at school that nobody likes a girl who is too smart. That means that I shouldn't do my work too good or really enjoy learning. I learned that the girls with nice figures who flirted a lot were more popular than the ones who had opinions. I started to keep quiet about things and I pretended to be pleasant and passive. To this very day, and I'm now 51 years old, I often find myself not saying what I really think when I am around a man. I usually pretend to like the things they like, think the way they think, and generally to be very passive—which I always thought was what men wanted me to be.

The specifics in these women's stories vary, but the undercurrent is the same—being married or committed to one man makes maintaining a separate identity, personal power, and one's special energy and rhythm impossible. While it is traditional and liberating to blame the man for this, women with a broader perspective recognize that it often has little to do with him specifically. Rather, responsibility may lie with the woman who enters the relationship desiring to play the role of wife and leaves it full of rage. The feminine reactor, who is totally out of touch with herself, is unable to see that she chose her male partner for the very same masculine qualities that, she later asserts, destroyed her identity, and that he paid a steep price too in terms of his feelings of being consumed, suffocated, and totally responsible for the well-being of his wife.

A pathetic, though powerfully telling, commentary on the end result of the we-think experience for women is a conclusion found in the research of Dr. Helena Z. Lopata, director of the Center for the Comparative Study of Social Roles at Loyola University of Chicago. She surveyed 301 widows (244 whites, 52 blacks, 5 unidentified) who were fifty years of age and over and who lived in metropolitan Chicago. Forty-two percent agreed that "I feel more independent and free now than before I became a widow," and in spite of financial and health problems, more than one out of three agreed that "this time of my life is actually easier than any other time."[7]

WE-THINK: HIS EXPERIENCE

The annihilation of separate identity and the stunting of growth as a result of the we-think phenomenon is less richly documented in the male, for a number of reasons. Perhaps the most critical is that the more he aspires to a state of masculine perfection (success, autonomy, dominance, rationality, invulnerability) the more machinelike he becomes and the more disconnected from his inner experience. He cannot feel, or fears acknowledging, his pain because he is rigidly locked in by his masculine defenses and sees no alternatives. The classic macho will tell you he "feels great" right until the day he drops dead of a heart attack. Overweight, alcoholic, and a chain smoker, he may know somewhere deep inside that he is in danger, but he can't really *feel* it, nor would he know how to go about changing himself.

Then again, his masculine posture of dominance, illusion of control, and feelings of responsibility result in self-hatred and guilt when things don't go as he'd want or expect. For example, contrast the earlier quotations from outraged women writers with these comments by a radical male physician and social commentator. Note his bias *toward* the woman and his hostile, blaming attitude toward his own sex.

But even the manipulation of pleasure is not the most horrendous feature of married life for women. The health of their bodies is the final broker in the distribution of power at home. . . .

Enhancing their husband's self-esteem is so deeply embedded a marital function that wives will actually get sick in order to allow their husbands to feel stronger and better then they. Since men frequently behave like babies in grown up bodies, women have to become very sick in order to be more disabled—sometimes they become paralyzed to let their husbands appear competent.

In more "primitive" societies, men actually perform clitoralectomies to make sure that women's capacity for pleasure does not interfere with their capacity for obedience. A more subtle and social form of the same procedure is performed in the modern American marriage. . . .[8]

Statistics often are cited to prove that marriage suits the husband better than it does his wife. This is probably true to the extent that it saves him from the terrible isolation and lack of intimacy that characterizes masculinity. His life as a work-machine provides few other human or personal compensations. Marriage also makes it possible for him to be comforted and fed by his wife-mother—important because his socialization has not included training him for self-care. His masculinity also demands he have a wife and children in order to prove that he is a man. The bargain traditionally entered into in marriage is that he acts as the provider in return for having his human needs taken care of. Is it any wonder that he is compulsively controlling and possessive of the woman, who is his human lifeline? It is the psychological tragedy of marriage that he makes a total emotional investment in a woman who is building up a mountain of rage toward him—someone who will likely feel freed and at her best when she is finally rid of him through divorce or his death.

The impact of we-think, the diminishing of the self within the traditional relationship, takes on a different form for men. They tend to become increasingly self-conscious, constricted, conservative, and work obsessed.

Women often can see the impact of we-think on their men more clearly than the men themselves. A twenty-five-year-old Latin American woman described the change her formerly fun-loving husband went through shortly after they married:

> Not long after the wedding, I noticed he never went anywhere except school and work. He didn't go out for rides on his bike and before long sold it because he wanted to increase our savings account. He became obsessed with money and the thought of not having enough. He became a television freak, especially during the weekends. This drove me out of the house. I tried to continue being active with him in sports and church, the both of which he put down. But he would just buy sports magazines and sit for hours playing statistical games with the batting averages the players had earned. He became very rigid and conservative, even to the point of dressing as if he were about forty instead of twenty-five. I know I could have made the marriage go on forever but I had no desire to do so. He lives in the future, always worrying about tomorrow. I wanted to live in the present and enjoy what there was to enjoy while I was young enough to do so, and not at some

mythical future time when he thought there was enough money and security to begin enjoying life.

Many married women have become disillusioned and have even been driven to distraction as their "devoted" husbands became increasingly dependent, to the point where they would go nowhere without their wives, and would follow them around the house desiring to be with them every moment. The facade of love concealed the reality of an oppressive possessiveness, offensive and terrorizing to the wife.

This kind of behavior may be due to the wife's negative reaction to any act of social independence on the man's part. It also stems from his feeling of being responsible for the well-being of a wife perceived as a helpless child. Finally, it results from his own terror of abandonment or rejection by her if he angers her, because he is deeply dependent on her.

Frank Armstrong was thirty-four years old when he left his wife to be with his "magic lady"—a young woman he claimed loved and understood him better than any other person he had ever known. He had been raised mainly in the streets and roamed freely from city to city for the first ten years of his adult life, before he became successful in sales promotion work. His lifestyle had been an expression of a powerful need to retain his own identity and rhythm, even during his seven-year marriage to his first wife.

Shortly after becoming attached to his new and "greatest" love, he experienced great guilt when he simply wanted to go off alone with a friend after work, needed time to be alone, or wanted to work late. When his new woman needed six weeks of hospitalization for major surgery soon after beginning to live with him, he said he felt relieved. He could now catch up on work, see friends, and do things he had denied himself during the time he had been transformed into a stay-at-home, television-watching, church-going "good boy."

When interviewed by a New York sociologist, several men articulated a similar feeling in their relationships. First, Tom: "When I was in an unofficial marriage with a woman, I would see only her and would be totally focused on her as the deciding factor of how my mood would be. It was a way of keeping myself out of having anything for myself and depriving myself of friends."[9]

Jim, who was divorced twice and has been living now as a single for five years, remarked, "I am having an experience I never had before, since I was always answerable to someone—my family or wife. I never had the experience of being completely self-motivated, of having to consider someone else's reaction to what I do—approval, disapproval, does the job pay enough? It makes me feel potent . . . and very responsible for what I do. Productive, capable of dealing with life's exigencies, and capable even of seeking friendly help when I need it. Whether you are self-realized or not cannot be blamed or credited to someone else."[10]

The married male often gets to the point where he no longer knows or can follow through on what he wants. He has substituted his wife's voice and desires for his own. While some women complain about their man's dependency on them, they directly and indirectly encourage it. A woman who has become sensitive to men's issues and problems reflected on her dissolved marriage: "I am ashamed to say I have often resented, and tried to discourage the hobbies and activities of my husband when we were married. I tagged along on the fishing and hunting trips he planned, somewhat reluctantly. Often I complained when he wanted to go off with his cronies to water ski or jeep ride or just to goof around. I selfishly wanted him all to myself and preferred less active things."

Perhaps men have not articulated the impact of we-think as powerfully as women because they don't really *expect* to feel good in a relatioship. They are focused on image, not process—how it looks rather than how it feels—because their prime need is to validate their masculinity. Having friends, feeling free and relaxed, and being playful is *not* what they expect. What it means to be a man is being able to take pressure and responsibility, not feeling good. *In that sense, the key difference between the man and the woman in relationships today is that he takes his oppression for granted, while she doesn't.*

TOOTHPASTE CAP FIGHTS AND WE-THINK

The resistance and irritation caused by we-think may be observed early on in most relationships via the phenomenon I call toothpaste cap fights. This term refers to disproportionate reactions and fights over minor incidents, such as a toothpaste cap left on the bathroom sink. These fights usually occur on a weekend morning or during a vacation, when the full, oppressive weight of relationship fusion is felt because the weekday escapes of work and busyness are not available. They are usually initiated by the man, who is irritable because he is feeling bored and trapped by guilt and unable to do what he really wants to do, which is to go off somewhere on his own.

These petty fights, therefore, tend to result in one partner, more often the man, stomping out of the house in righteous indignation. He now has a "good" reason for doing what he really wanted all along but couldn't have otherwise done because of guilt. These arguments are later followed by sentimental apologizing and earnest resolves to "make love, not war," and to be more patient in the future. The resolutions are, however, very short-lived because the toothpaste cap fights are not seen for what they are—unconscious attempts to separate oneself and break out of the suffocation of we-think.

Typically, in the name of being loving, partners abandon their capacity to state simply, "I want to be alone," or even more threateningly, "I want to be with someone else." Saying this would result in guilt, hurt feelings, and fears of rejection. Instead, therefore, a progressive loss of identity boundaries occur.

This leads to a conflict that rarely gets resolved. That is, both partners tend to fear separateness and possible abandonment more than they cherish retaining their separate sense of self. Therefore, instead of arriving at a resolution, they embark on a never-ending series of toothpaste cap fights, a safety valve allowing one or both to temporarily escape.

The pressure of we-think progressively contaminates and undermines all of the joys and potentials of intimacy, as it becomes more difficult to differentiate what is being done out of genuine desire and what is a reflex reaction emerging from this fusion. Couples who are "in love" begin to sleep together in the same bed; telephone each other during the day; engage in conversation, eat meals, and spend weekends together automatically; and develop feelings of guilt and fear when they don't feel like engaging each other in these ways.

Among more thoroughly socialized and self-controlled couples, where the we-think phenomenon does not ignite direct, raging encounters or overt violence, it may arouse secret desires for one's partner to take sick or die in an accident so that one can be free. Thus there emerges the fantasy of being released without guilt via some twist of fate.

THE SOCIAL EXPERIENCE AND WE-THINK

Traditional couples know the boredom of socializing with another couple. After such get-togethers, it is common for each couple to gossip about and denigrate the other, and even comment on how dull they were.

Parties made up of married couples tend to be predictable—matters of drinking liquor, eating excessively, and making strained conversation sprinkled with dreary joke telling, especially by the men. The energy, if it is there at all, comes from the secret flirting that often goes on.

Each partner in a couple, when encountered alone, may have a sparkle, playfulness, and adventurous vitality that seems to disappear when they socialize together. Both become diminished and predictable.

Reflecting on his married years, one man in his late thirties commented:

"When I divorced after seven years of a traditional relationship, I found that I had no desire to continue my relationship with the married couples that my wife and I had socialized with during our marriage. Looking back, it seems clear that the couples we socialized with had been unconsciously chosen because they were 'safe.' That is, they had the same materialistic preoccupations and personally repressed styles we had. Few of the couples, including ourselves, had unmarried friends, unless they were lonely, isolated, 'loser' types who, by their seeming unhappiness, validated the wisdom of our union."

The price of the "security" that the we-think fusion facilitates is constriction rather than growth, isolation rather than openness to new relationships, guilt rather than spontaneity, predictability rather than risk, passivity rather than activity in the interaction, and materialism rather than pleasure in personal experiences.

There are no secret, magic answers to the critical question of how to avoid the we-think trap. It is the defensive, inevitable result of the bonding of two people who need each other and yet have little in common on an objective, here-and-now basis. The more balanced or complete each partner is upon entering the relationship, so that the attraction is based on genuine mutual liking and stimulation rather than on fantasies generated by need, the less will the phenomenon of we-think appear.

PART TWO

TRANSITION

6 Driving Each Other Crazy on the Way to Liberation

AMBIVALENCE in the man-woman relationship in this era of women's and men's liberation seems commonplace. Intense passion, euphoria, and commitment are followed by withdrawal into oneself, intellectualizing, threatening, or severing the relationship; the pattern is one of coming close, then backing away. We emerge like wounded, self-protective children from our safe corners, just long enough to test our latest fantasy and to momentarily risk being open and vulnerable. More often than not we retreat feeling wounded again and disillusioned.

Those who are in a committed relationship fantasize leaving and being "free" again. They find their emotions and responses toward their partners swinging between extremes: they feel close then totally distant, loving then hateful, with warm attraction changing into cold detachment, insecure clinging becoming defensive autonomy. Those who are unattached find endless reasons not to get emotionally involved with the latest possible partner.

The ideologies of liberation are a major element in producing this "crazymaking" ambivalence. In a time of awakening to the issues, we come to see the problems and the theoretical solutions intellectually, but our intellectual vision is advanced far beyond our emotional development. As a result our intellectual awareness demands a form of relationship that is often in complete contradiction to our deeper cravings and capacities.

Thus, when one part of oneself is satisfied, another part feels deprived, threatened, or resentful. Nothing feels completely right or enough, so we drive each other and ourselves crazy with double messages and conflicting expectations. We ask for something, then react negatively when we get it. "Don't treat me like a child, but take care of me!" she says. "Be independent, but need me!" is his refrain.

Writer Phyllis Raphael disclosed, "I am tired of being a lonely, self-reliant adult. I am bored with liberation. I am fed up with sexual freedom and sick to death of a life without commitment. . . . I am no longer able to live by the old rules, but I cannot find any new ones that work either, and it is driving me crazy. What the answer is I do not know, but I am beginning to believe I am too frightened ever to love anyone again, and that scares me more than words can say. I am a lonely, self-reliant adult. Quite frankly, I despise it."[1]

An article recently published on the contemporary male's dilemma expressed a comparable mood: "These are dark days for love. . . . Today there is heat without adhesion. Men and women circle each other, wrestlers on guard, costumed and self-conscious. . . . [They] fall to the mat—in an embrace or a headlock, depending on whose side you're on. It is over in seconds. Next! . . . It used to happen some other way, didn't it?"

The male writer concludes, "He knows that if he waits much longer, that if he doesn't soon find this woman, his years will be filled with no more than a series of fast-fading images. . . . His life will be no life at all."[2]

This driving yourself and others crazy on the way to liberation is painful, yet natural in a period of transition. On the one hand, it seems inherent in the human experience to be constantly pulled between the poles of security and desire for growth, between intimacy needs and the lust for freedom. It is also in the nature of an intellectualized society such as ours that we are torn between our emotions and our expectations and attitudes. The many variations on the theme might include the "liberated" woman who still blames men for all her problems just like the traditional woman, or the "liberated" man who deludes himself into believing that he is giving up some control when he tells his lover to take the initiative sexually tonight. There is the woman who claims both the rights of liberation and the prerogative of being put first because she's a woman; and the man who discusses his feelings, but in an intellectual way. There is the "liberated" woman who creates and uses the aura of being assertive, independent, and sexual to make herself more attractive to men in order to more rapidly achieve the traditional goal of getting married to a successful man and being taken care of. She exposes her true motives and her facade of being liberated when, on failing to reach her goal of marriage or exclusivity, she angrily abandons a relationship she ostensibly was involved in for its own sake, and not to get a husband. Her counterpart is the "liberated, gentle" man who uses a facade of warmth, sensitivity, eye contact, and "understanding the woman's plight" to gain the traditional masculine goal of seduction more easily and less expensively than he could were he playing by traditional rules. He exposes his true motives when he quickly pulls away from the relationship after he has accomplished his goal or been denied it.

Contradictions and hypocrisies, conscious and otherwise, abound. In addition, what we believe is our visionary intellectual awareness may simply be a defensive denial of opposite feelings inside ourselves, rather than a genuinely humanistic impulse. Much of liberation rhetoric contains a protesting-too-much quality that deserves a skeptical response. It encloses and narrows, rather than opening and expanding.

True growth is largely a gradual, even imperceptible, nonintellectual process. Hence the gap between "enlightened" attitudes and less conscious emotional reactions is probably largest in those who make their leaps into "awareness" dramatically and rapidly—the result of a "click experience" coming as a powerful defensive reaction against the painful strictures of one's past, rather than developing out of an objective perspective and a slow, genuine growth process leading to wholeness. They develop counter-defenses to their original gender defenses. Genuine closeness becomes almost, if not totally, impossible, as every response is eventually found objectionable and every person of the opposite sex is found wanting.

Conflicting messages between the sexes, therefore, become the norm in this time of transition. We move rapidly between reaching out and pulling away, depending on whether our minds or our emotions are prevailing. Defensive protections against this confusion develop and they make our intimate man-woman encounters progressively more unstable and short-lived. If Los Angeles, where I live, is any indication, the total coupling sequence, from excitement to boredom to rage, which used to take years, is now often being played out in the span of one weekend.

THE WAYS *SHE* DRIVES *HIM* CRAZY

Torn between her old and new selves, the woman reviles and mocks the sexist macho, but then finds herself equally offended by the man who is consciously working to liberate himself in order to be what she claims to want. Repulsed by the "liberated" male, she may find, suddenly and confusingly to herself and others, that Mr. Macho begins to look good again. She protests the lack of emotional expressiveness and vulnerability in the male, but, as one woman in a moment of unadorned truth said, "I'm so sick of the bleeding-heart men who want to tell you how they feel all the time—to 'share themselves.' God, I start to miss the old-time guy who kept his feelings to himself."

Child care and the sharing of this responsibility is a major issue for the emerging woman. Here again, however, the man who buys into this demand for major involvement in the child-raising process might find himself receiving subtle or even direct communications of resentment. Feminist Robin Morgan articulated the basis for this sentiment: "Motherhood is the one area where *we're* raised to have some power, and sure, we're ambivalent about sharing it." Describing her own experience of letting her husband care for their infant son while she was on a lecture tour, she said, "You *do* regret that someone else was there when the baby took his first step."[3]

Well-known writer Jane Howard traveled cross-country to research her book on women. She was sometimes accompanied by her lover. On the trip, he was in the supportive role traditionally played by women who accompany their men on business trips. "While she interviews and leaps from place to place he sightsees, museum hops, waits in hotel rooms for her return. Mostly they do not get along well and the irony of role reversal escapes nobody. She is hypercritical; he cannot drive a car and she cannot stand it. She doesn't realize, however, that her own clashing needs and sensibilities are one of the more poignant themes of the book—the dilemma of the self-governing woman whose extreme competence only makes her more intolerant of her man's shortcomings. After all, the confusion wails, he's a man and he *should* be smarter, stronger, better than I. Autonomy vs. take-care-of-me. Surely a contemporary dilemma" was the way the female writer analyzed it.[4]

One forty-seven-year-old man, embittered by what he felt were the hypocritical responses of his own wife and other women he knew, wrote the following:

One of the things that I have learned about people over the years is that they lie a great deal. You can't go by what they say—only on what

they do. You say that "women are eager to see
men change." They might say this to you but I
invite you to look at the reality. The macho man
is still the man who gets the most pussy. Women—
especially the feminists—talk and talk about the
man who can cry, who is in touch with his
emotions, etc., but the guy they climb into bed
with is the guy with the fewest feminine characteristics. Actually, it would seem as if the arrow of
evolution itself is inexorably pointed in the direction of macho. Since the macho man is going to
get more pussy than the non-macho, his characteristics are more likely to be perpetuated since he
is going to have more children. Also, whether he
is around or not, his children will be raised by a
mother who admires macho and will steer her
sons in that direction.

Women want to mate with men who have power
or the appearance of it. While it is rare that non-
macho types have power, it is possible and has
happened—largely through accidents of royal birth
in the past and bureaucratic staying power in the
present. I have the impression that these kinds of
freaks are able to get few women in spite of their
power. One reads of the effete nobleman whose
conjugal duties are taken over by a gardener, etc.

Several weeks ago, my wife to whom I've been
married for 21 years and I were in a restaurant
late at night. Some young punk made some remarks to her. She never did tell me exactly what
he said. She demanded that I take action. Well,
yes, I scared the hell out of him and he ran away.
Do you think I enjoyed my meal? I shook all the
way through it. I expected a gang of guys to be
waiting when we got out. All through the meal I

fingered my pocket knife and planned street-fight strategy. Nothing happened. Do I like the macho role? Hell, no! But what else is there? I will play any role my wife wants me to play. This year she passed me in income. She can drive better than I can. She can operate any machinery I can operate. But I still am the one she looks to for protection.

Actually, when you talk about less macho, you are simply saying that young men should act more like old men. Do women really want this? Not on your life!

Perhaps the dilemma many men find themselves in today is most graphically reflected in a comment by a woman who was leaving her husband. In desperation, he asked her, "If I change the way I am, can we make it?" to which she replied, "My list of resentments would only grow in a new way."

Some women seem to transcend this time of confusion by making a leap into macho defenses. They rigidly deny their dependency, emotions, and fears. Then they pay the price that men do—loneliness, a driven goal-oriented lifestyle, and a lack of sensitivity to their impact on the men who flee from relationships with them.

As female machos, they experience the world much the same way as the masculine male. They protest that they have it as bad as the contemporary man, and indeed they do. Macho can exist in male or female. It is a set of defense mechanisms against experiencing and acknowledging needs, vulnerability, dependency, fear, passivity, emotion. The sum of these defenses is detached, dehumanized behavior. A woman, therefore, can be just as macho as a man, and, by the same token, a man can have feminine defenses. *It is the effect of these masculine and feminine defenses that produces interpersonal problems and distortions in awareness, not a person's gender.*

A group of men, at a communications lab for men and women interested in working toward a new man-woman relationship, confronted the women with the no-win situation they felt themselves to be in:

> You want to be related to as a separate, autonomous person and yet be taken care of at the same time. If we take you at face value and relate to you completely as an equal, you feel resentful and frustrated. If we cater to you in traditional ways, you say you feel demeaned and offended.
>
> You want us to be intimate and deeply connected to you in a relationship. If we get attached, you start feeling bored, unchallenged and engulfed, and tell us we're getting too dependent. If we resist, we are accused of being immature, narcissistic, and fearful of commitment.
>
> You want to be related to as a person, not a sex object, but then you're attracted to men according to their occupational status—their positions of power and their wealth. When we relate to you in kind, you pull away in resentment and disappointment, blaming us and labeling us chauvinists.
>
> You want us to show feelings, but, on a deeper level, you still associate our display of emotion with weakness. If we show emotion, you find us weak. If the emotions are ones you don't like, such as anger, jealousy, dependency, or neediness, you accuse us of being hostile or troubled. If we control our feelings, you say we're defensive and closed.

You resent and reject any expectations that you take primary responsibility for domestic chores. Yet you still see us as the ones primarily responsible for financial support. When we do make great efforts to share in domestic responsibilities, you get critical of our competence and tend to discourage us because you say that we're intruding. If we're not good and steady providers, you lose respect and attraction for us as "men."

If we make major decisions without consulting you, you feel controlled. If we don't make the decisions, or put the responsibility in your lap, you see us as indecisive and unsure of ourselves.

If we don't hang out with male friends, you say you want us to, and even complain that we're always underfoot. If we do have close friends and we invest time and emotion in such relationships, you complain of being neglected and suggest that our behavior is immature and even suggestive of latent homosexuality.

If we're sexually aggressive, you react negatively to our "demanding, pressuring behavior." If we aren't sexually aggressive or wait for you to do your share of the initiation of sex, you see us as ineffectual, passive, unmasculine lovers.

You want us to be more sexually relaxed and sensual and less goal driven and performance conscious. Yet you're upset and wonder what's wrong when we don't have an erection. You still expect us to be fine sexual performers.

You encourage us to work less, but you don't make concrete proposals on ways to spend less money. If we continue to work hard, you see us as obsessed with money, success and ambition, and avoiding the relationship. If we start to play more and work less, we get overwhelmed with the anxiety and responsibility of being the primary support for the family because you're not really taking up enough of the slack.

You complain about the lack of communication. When we say, "Okay, let's try. What do you want to talk about?" you say, "I don't know. You start."

You tell us you want to know when we're angry. If we do risk expressing strong angry reactions, you respond by withdrawing, crying, blaming, and accusing us of being hostile and insensitive.

If we're dominant in the relationship, you say we're being controlling. If we give up being dominant, often nothing happens because you don't fill the vacuum, and you see us as being weak.

If we say we want to be nurtured and taken care of, you see us as dependent and demanding. If we resist being vulnerable by not revealing our needs, you say we're afraid of exposing ourselves and getting close.

You say you want us to be spontaneous and real in interacting with you. If we are, however, and "being real" includes behavior and language that you don't like or you consider to be sexist, you become critical and judgmental of us. You're really telling us that you want us to be "real," but only in ways that please you.

You want us to be ambitious and successful, but still be relaxed, intimate and connected. You want us to be the "best of all possible worlds" in a way that it is impossible. You want a warm, intimate being and a world-beater all rolled up in one, and that doesn't exist.

THE WAYS *HE* DRIVES *HER* CRAZY

The history of men driving women crazy with double messages on their path to liberation is briefer and less well documented because the women's movement and changes have a twenty-year history, while men's consciousness raising has only begun recently. Even the awareness of any need for change is still being resisted by many men.

Whereas women's conflicts leading to crazymaking responses center on issues of taking control, being direct and assertive, owning their sexuality, and expressing aggression, men's conflicts are founded in the opposite issues. Men on the way to liberation are trying to discover *how to let go* of rigid tendencies to control and be autonomous, unemotional, unneeding, aggressive, sexually driven, and invulnerable, while at the same time retaining a sense of safety, of being appropriately masculine, attractive to women, and respected by men and women alike.

On a deeper level still, a man may want to free himself up, yet hold on to the excitement his masculine orientation provides him through continuous challenges and battles. Furthermore, his desire to see the woman change and become an equal partner conflicts with a reluctance to lose the power and control over her that he feels guarantees her attachment and continuing interest.

Unlike the contemporary women who feel that their growth takes precedence over their relationship with a man, most men fear changing in a way that will jeopardize their attractiveness to a woman. This, of course, is the key difference in the quality and quantity of women's and men's attempts at change today. Psychologically, he is significantly

more isolated and less capable of forming meaningful relationships than she, and therefore significantly
more dependent on her, in the deepest sense, than
she is on him. Because *he needs her significantly
more than she needs him, he fears changing in a
way that might alienate her.*

As he struggles to change, he drives her crazy
with his own contradictory messages. He conveys
that he wants a woman to be strong, independent,
and assertive, but then becomes romantically attracted to the woman who plays the traditional feminine games of being adoring and submissive. This
bind was expressed cogently by a woman who had
worked hard and honestly to become everything a
desirable yet autonomous person should be. She
was self-reliant yet nurturing and caring, the kind of
woman who could head a corporation and still love
being at home with her children. She said "So, now
he says I've become *too much* for him. When I'm
passive, I'm boring. When I'm strong, I'm too threatening."

A twenty-eight-year-old, unmarried professional
woman described the disappointment she felt with
a man she was beginning to become fond of:

> On a recent trip I was on, an interesting inci-
> dent happened. The first night that we went out
> to dinner we ate at a very expensive restaurant.
> Cliff picked up the tab for it. The second night,
> we also ate in a very expensive restaurant. When
> it came time to pay the bill I said, "I'd like to pay
> for dinner tonight." He made a very mild protest
> and then he let me pay. If he had really pushed
> the point, I wouldn't have gotten him into an
> embarrassing situation. I'd have let him pay for

the dinner and talked to him about it later. But he didn't. I thought that it was really neat that somebody with a lot of traditional views could let this happen, and I was going to compliment him about it later.

I got home and I opened up my cigarette case and there was the money for the dinner that he had slipped in. The first thought I had was that it was very much like something my father would do to me when I was a little girl. He'd let me pay for something, and later I'd find the money somewhere. . . . It's something that you do that's nice for a little child, but it's not something that you do for an adult person that y 'u respect. It's not just how men see women. It's how they are refusing to see women too that I think is equally as important.

A married woman in the process of investing considerable time and energy in her career found herself experiencing intense anger over the bind she found herself in. "I'm expected to be affectionate, devoted to my family, and at the same time I know that society doesn't put much value on that, though they pay some lip service to it. If I'm not constantly affectionate, close, and loving, then I'm a failure as a woman. If I do make that my primary thing, then I'm taken for granted and considered a failure as a person. Periodically, when I get in touch with what's happening, I can barely contain the rage I feel inside me over being trapped like this."

The dominant, excruciating threat to women involves the struggle to develop their autonomous strength and yet retain their lovability and attractiveness to men, and to themselves. They experience the hypocritical reactions of men who praise them yet hotly pursue the old-time *femme fatale*. Small wonder many become embittered, like the sensitive man who finds himself being ignored by women.

One woman writer called these "perilous times—women will have to stick it out, learn to survive the fear that independence and self-definition can only be had at the expense of love and warmth."[5]

Dr. Robert Tucker, associate professor of psychiatry at Yale University, who along with his psychologist wife, Dr. Leotta Tucker, developed "Black love" workshops to help close the gap between black men and women, described the double-bind the strong black woman finds herself in today: "Men often commend black women for their strength, but their admiration is not demonstrated in the ways they relate to women. They resent black women for not being soft and submissive. In a sense, they are asking women to be all things."[6]

Dr. A. Poussaint, a Harvard psychiatrist, also commented on the black man's attitude toward strong women: "Men get upset when women seem to be competitive with them in every day kinds of ways, by challenging them, by testing their personhood, their self-esteem, touching off insecurities, when there seems always to be some one-upmanship going on in the relationship."[7]

Women at the communications lab previously referred to in this chapter confronted the men with the no-win situation they were finding themselves placed in by them:

> You tell us you want us to be directly, assertively, and openly sexual and then you become passive, intimidated, and rejecting when we do.

If we're directly sexual, you're turned off or threatened by the absence of challenge and seduction, even though you tell us you like the honesty. If we're less sexually available, you accuse us of playing games.

You want us to take responsibility, pay for ourselves, and not lean on you for support. Yet you're threatened and resentful if that process takes us away from you in terms of time, emotional involvement, or our need for you. In other words, you want us to have our own means of support, but to treat our jobs as if they were avocations that did not take anything away from you. You don't want our independence to develop to the point where we're no longer dependent on you, because you're afraid we may come to realize that we don't need or even like you at all.

If we're available to you and cater to your needs, you take us for granted and even lose respect for us. If we don't attend to you, you accuse us of being selfish and rejecting.

You want us to handle our outside work without expressing frustrations or feelings about it. You lecture us about the ways of the world and on how to be more objective, pragmatic, and self-serving. If we listen to you and adopt that style and become ambitious and successful, you call us cold, "ballbreakers," and "unfeminine."

You want us to take responsibility for decisions and for structuring the time when we're together. When we do, and we tell you what we've planned, you react critically because our plans are different from what you would have planned, or you're just uninterested. If we don't make decisions or plans, you attack us for not taking responsibility, for being boring, and for lacking imagination.

You tell us you want us to know what makes us angry and to express that to you directly. When we do, you accuse us of being hostile, rejecting, judgmental, and castrating. If we withhold the anger, you accuse us of being phony and manipulative, and you don't really trust us.

You want us to be more objective and logical in our approach to the relationship. When we are, you call us unfeeling, uncaring, or too detached. If we don't, you get exasperated by our "irrationality" and accuse us of being "crazy."

You want to be the central person in our lives. When you are, you feel we're too demanding of your time and energy. When we don't center our lives around you, you accuse us of being unloving and rejecting.

You want us to take care of ourselves physically, to be active and in shape. At the same time, you don't like it if you think we're going to become "jocks" or athletically competitive. If we become more athletic, you begin to relate to us as a buddy and become less attracted to us sexually. You start to look at the passive, "frail" woman on the sidelines, with her makeup and high heels, who thinks you're Superman because she's so uncoordinated. If we don't stay in shape, you accuse us of being lazy and letting ourselves go.

You say you want the relationship to be more playful and interesting. When we get really playful and loosen up, you look really uncomfortable and try to shut us down.

PARTNERS DRIVING EACH OTHER CRAZY

Striving for a liberated, equal relationship ("close but free and equal") that, at the same time, guarantees all the benefits and security of the traditional relationship as at the root of volatile, fragile, crazy-making couple interactions. He says, "I meet a 'strong' woman. The moment we get emotionally involved, however, she turns into a little girl who gives up her identity and wants to be taken care of." She says, "I meet a 'liberated' man. The moment we get involved, he wants to possess and control me; and when I give him what he says he wants—someone to love him and still let him be—he backs off and disappears."

A classic arena for such conflicting messages is sexuality. He says he wants her to be more directly sexual, and she professes to want that too. Yet when she is, he feels put upon and she wonders whether she is making herself too easily available. Further, his casual response to her new sexuality makes her feel undesirable. Being directly sexual also means abandoning a traditional source of power for her. She becomes resentful if he seems to take sex with her for granted. She tells him he doesn't have to feel pressured to perform, yet reacts negatively to his lack of an erection or arousal. He also becomes threatened and feels pressured when she begins to expect orgasms and slow, sensual lovemaking, and it tends to tense him up. He tells her he wants her to be sexual but gets aroused more by her unavailability.

In their relationship in general, they tend to become increasingly self-conscious and consequently immobilized with each other, fearful of pressuring

each other and resentful of anything that suggests a
sexist expectation. Her defensiveness about sexism
makes it increasingly more difficult for him to ask
for what he wants, even though she may tell him to
be direct. He fears she will see him as demanding or
as putting her in a subservient role. Likewise, she
wants to be more direct and open but fears that she
will offend him. So each withholds needs and feelings, and deep-seated resentments over giving but
not getting develop. In addition, each wants growth
and change in the other, but with no threat to his or
her own security.

Michael and Debby Richards are a contemporary
couple, in a volatile relationship because of these
endlessly conflicting messages and impulses. They
live in a small, growing community in Colorado
that is rooted traditionally, yet is very much a part
of the stream of new awareness about the roles of
men and women.

Debby is a competition-caliber skier and part-time
carpenter. Michael is a computer salesman with a
quiet, introspective, and sensitive manner. Torn between their traditional-rooted needs and their newly
awakened desires for liberation, they were driving
each other crazy, to the point of repeated major
fights in which divorce was threatened, when they
consulted a therapist to help them with their relationship.

Debby, now thirty, became the mother of two
children in her early twenties and had to leave
college, but since developed an independent lifestyle.
After several years she returned to school, and spent
many hours at skiing practice and exercising to stay
in condition, coming home at erratic hours. This
meant that, though her husband was providing their

sole financial support, he often had to prepare meals for himself and the children. Debby was insistent that her husband not have traditional wifely expectations of her and that he be supportive of her educational and athletic endeavors. She would tell him, "You got me pregnant when I was young so I couldn't finish school."

Michael, a driven businessman, was searching for ways to lighten his schedule so he could spend more time with friends and also study music. And he felt deeply hurt that his wife was seldom there to greet him or make dinner when he returned home from work.

Arguments would break out regularly as she insisted Michael was trying to control her and force her into the role of old-fashioned wife. He countered that she didn't really care about him.

Heated exchanges would also take place regarding decision making. They were selling their home and building a new one, so they needed to find a place to live in the interim. Debby would resist assuming responsibility for relocating. Michael would fume that she expected him to do everything. She would counter that whenever she did make decisions, as he requested, he was always critical of her choices. When he took the matter of relocation in hand (Debby had said, "You take care of it. Just move us in"), she resented him for not consulting her before the final decision.

Both acknowledged their interest in others sexually, but denied having had affairs. Jealousy and suspicion built until they finally decided to reveal their sexual fantasies to each other. When Debby described hers about other men they both knew, Michael acted hurt and angry. When she became reluctant to continue the discussion, he accused her, "You're holding back stuff. I don't trust you. You don't level with me."

Equally painful fights would break out over the rearing of their hyperactive daughter. Michael would accuse Debby of ignoring the girl or overprotecting her, to which Debby would counter, "You take care of her, then," whereupon Michael would call her an irresponsible mother.

Therapy for this couple required over a year of work on taking responsibility and not blaming, recognizing the double-binds they put each other in, and separating out their deeper emotional responses from their more advanced intellectual ideas about what a liberated marriage should be.

Another variation on partners' driving each other crazy with inconsistent and contradictory expectations involved a recently married couple in their late thirties who had descended from a euphoric, "magical" courtship to near violence within six months of marriage. Both had already been divorced, in order to escape very traditional marriages, and vowed never to get tied into such a structure again. Within three hours of meeting at a singles vacation resort, Victoria told Matt that she was "hot for him" and wanted to make love. Matt reacted with delight at her directness and they had passionate sex for the rest of the day. Matt was in awe of Victoria's casual use of "vulgar language" and her aggressiveness combined with womanly charm. He also admired her casual attitude toward spending money. She was the "live life to the fullest" woman he'd been looking for after fifteen years of a very traditional marriage to an "uptight, conventional woman who didn't know how to have fun."

At the time of their meeting Matt was unemployed and not looking seriously for a job. Instead, he lived on his meager savings and spent his days practicing piano and writing in his journal. Victoria thought that his relaxed attitude toward work was wonderful.

A month later, they decided to marry, convinced that each had found a "magic" person in the other. However, within three months, Matt began reacting negatively to Victoria's frank language and her "ostentatious, sexy" clothing. These were the same things that had originally delighted him about this "far-out liberated lady," as he used to describe her. Now he was calling her a foul-mouthed slut, and accusing her of acting seductive toward every attractive man she saw. He tore up and threw away the bikini that he had loved so much the day they met. He also began to criticize her for her spendthrift habits. Though she had always prided herself on her independence, she deferred to his criticism and tried to change to please him.

Victoria meanwhile was becoming increasingly irritated at Matt's passive attitude toward finding a job and his always being underfoot at their apartment. She became enraged when he went clothes shopping with her credit card.

Prior to the marriage, Matt had had numerous friends and acquaintances. Victoria had admired him for having close male friends. After the wedding, she acted suspicious and hurt when he went off to spend a day with his buddies. She called him a "latent homo" and wondered why he'd still be interested in being with his bachelor friends.

Victoria would alternate between acting tough and independent, then crying like a hurt little girl. Matt would alternate between being the macho husband-master and acting like a dependent little boy. Whichever role either played, it eventually became a source of conflict, and the fights became progressively more explosive till they reached the point of violence. These people were hopelessly entangled in the conflict between their old traditional selves and their new selves, when they decided to divorce.

Having one foot in tradition and the other in a vision of a liberated relationship, "open, honest, free, and spontaneous," many couples drive each other crazy with these contradictory expectations. The major areas of such conflicts are:

Grow (Change)
BUT
Don't Threaten My Security

Feeling expansive, secure, and optimistic, partners provide mutual encouragement to develop and change. Feeling insecure and rejected, they fear the same changes as threats to the relationship, at which time attempts are made to undermine the other person's development. If one changes, the other is threatened. When changes stop, threat turns to boredom.

Be Open and Honest
BUT
Don't Be Insensitive and Hurtful

There is a desire in every liberation-minded couple to be totally honest, to avoid the hypocrisy of being intimate and deceitful at the same time. Truth and directness can be hurtful or threatening, however. If this weren't true, the information and feedback wouldn't have been withheld in the first place. When there is openness, the other person is likely to feel hurt. If openness is avoided, there are accusations of being dishonest.

Be Free
BUT
Be Close

The hunger to be close but free is one of the most powerful forms of liberation crazymaking. The fantasy such couples have is one of intense intimacy coupled with complete freedom. Double-bind messages become rampant in this atmosphere. Accusations of engulfment and desires for freedom are followed by screams of outraged pain over feeling rejected and abandoned whenever either partner behaves autonomously.

Be Yourself
BUT
Be Appropriate and Realistic

This is the conflict between the desire to have one's partner "be real" and the desire for him or her to accommodate any changes to one's own limitations. Either way, resentment builds. Being real may provoke feelings of rejection in one's partner. The accommodation of one's changes to the limits and anxieties of the partner leads to a sense of being controlled by the latter.

Express Your True Feelings
BUT
Express Only Those Feelings That Fit My Image of You

When women and men encourage each other to share real feelings, they often really mean only those feelings that are controllable and do not impair the romantic image. Women tell men to feel free to cry or express hurt or pain, but seem to forget that being honest about feelings includes the expression of unattractive emotions and responses, including boredom, rage, confusion, jealousy, and possessiveness. These negative emotions tend to be interpreted as neurotic and hostile when they are openly expressed. Likewise, when women are open about the full range of their impulses and feelings—including boredom, horniness, resistance to playing the womanly role, interest in other men—they're met with defensive hostility.

LIBERATION PHILOSOPHY AS DISGUISED RAGE

Single men who say that all liberated women are hypocrites wanting the best of both worlds; liberated single women who say there are no good men left; feminists who are defensive and suspicious of men no matter what they do (if he's macho, he's a sexist; if he's trying to liberate himself, he's a phony) and who cloak their hostility in the abstractions and polemics of liberation philosophy; people who passionately cherish their autonomy, not allowing anyone to intrude on their space—all may be rationalizing, channeling, and thereby controlling intense internal rage toward the opposite sex. Their liberation philosophies become the means by which they transform this rage into acceptable and "enlightened" philosophical positions. While maintaining that they desire intimacy under the right conditions, they never seem to find those conditions or to meet anyone who is perfect enough. Their underlying repressed rage creates the detachment and carping that put members of the opposite sex on the defensive and make it impossible for anybody to get close without being psychologically dissected and humiliated.

In an age of transition such as we are in today, the psychological challenge is to separate out what is articulated philosophically from the emotional intent underneath it. When is a philosophical position about liberation to be taken literally, and when is it an unconsciously disguised attempt at one-upmanship designed to bludgeon the opposite sex? In the latter case, others are repeatedly placed in a position where no matter what they do (except perhaps die or disappear), they're wrong, failing, or suspect. The desire for intimacy may be expressed, but the underlying motivation is to wall oneself in and keep relationships away. A posture of constantly blaming others and the injustices of society is taken.

This can be equally true for either men or women who are involved in their own "liberation changes." The "click experience" that feminists originally defined as the moment of sudden enlightenment about sexism, an experience that many men today are also having, while being initially exhilarating and freeing, may symbolically represent the clicking of the gate to forever bar that feared intimacy with the opposite sex. The liberation philosophy thus becomes a rigid, tight system that tolerates no new or dissonant information that could alter the "enlightened" point of view. It creates permanent insulation by putting the individual behind an intricate intellectual defense structure, even though a conscious desire for intimacy is expressed.

In this sense, the newly liberated person resembles the religious fanatics who believe they are trying to enlighten and help, but who succeed only in driving others away by confronting them with their "sinful," or in this case "sexist," ways. Isolating themselves is the unconscious and ultimate intent of such liberationists. The overt message they articulate may be humanistic but the emotional tone behind it is critical, righteous, judgmental, hostile, and distancing. They cut themselves off progressively from all those who resist becoming similarly enlightened. After a while, however, they find reasons to disagree even with those who seem to hold basically the same philosophies as they do, but whom they come to see as hypocrites or as not being dedicated enough. They are left isolated on top of their own liberation mountain. Their philosophies are revealed as disguises—as barriers used to keep intimate contact away, to deny and control their own dangerous rage, and to affirm their superiority.

Much of contemporary double-binding must be viewed in this light in order to be understood. Nothing you do is right because the underlying intent of the other person is to maintain an impenetrable wall. These are men and women who have been so wounded by intimate encounters in this time of transition that they have become suspicious, defensive, and enraged. In some cases they may also fear being cannibalized by intimacy, and other threatening fantasies projected onto the opposite sex. Consequently, trying to break through their wall is exhausting and usually futile.

A common illusion is that intimacy can be had between two people who share the same philosophy about liberation and nonsexist relationships. This is a fallacy based on the confusion of process (how two people relate) with content (the philosophy they share). It is an ultimate crazymaker because of the strong feeling each has that "we *should* be able to make this relationship work because we have the same values and attitudes about roles and relationships." Sharing similar abstract ideas about liberation, however, is rarely an adequate basis for intimacy if one is "falling in love" with a philosophy that emerges from the defenses against rage and resistances to intimacy of the other. Consequently, the relationship evolves into a cold, analytic, mutually judgmental standoff.

These two people circle, observe, analyze, and criticize each other to exhaustion. Each eventually becomes disillusioned because the other isn't what he or she "pretended" to be, and the relationship "doesn't feel good anymore." Both are left with a sense of betrayal and even greater anger, disillusionment, and self-protectiveness.

Relationships are lived and defined in process ("how we feel being together"), not in content ("we both cook and enjoy playing racquetball"). In the case of the "liberated" couple, the shared ideas about relationships are often attractive and abstractly perfect, but the process between the two on a moment-to-moment basis is intellectualized, controlled, cautious, and joyless. Trying to improve the relationship by tinkering with the content only intensifies the crazymaking.

How can one determine when a liberation philosophy is defensive, a displacement of disguised rage designed to isolate the person behind a wall of superiority? If the philosophy is a cover for disguised rage . . .

- There is a tendency to think in terms of "All men are . . ." or "All women are . . ." and the only exceptions made are for those of the opposite sex who hold a philosophy identical to one's own. Eventually, those people too are found to be ideologically flawed.
- There is a sense of hopelessness about ever making a relationship work because of the supposed absence of suitably liberated partners of the opposite sex.
- When a relationship begins to sour, the philosophy or values of the other person are blamed. Frequently, there is disillusionment over the fact that the other person didn't live up to the ideals he or she espoused and wasn't the person advertised.
- In discussing philosophical beliefs about liberation with someone who holds an opposing position, there is a tendency to become irritated and to rapidly reach the boiling point, bringing an end to the discussion.
- The liberation philosophy is basically impenetrable by those with opposing ideas or information. Nothing another says seems to ever change the way of thinking or alter philosophical convictions.
- There is an attraction to literature, drama, poetry, films, and art that support the favored point of view, while ignoring, depreciating, or condemning any contrary artistic expression.
- In moods of "clarity," there is a tendency to believe the absolute worst about the opposite

sex, e.g., "All men are rapists," "All women are manipulators and exploiters."

- The slightest, mildly offensive remark or behavior by a person one is involved with can transform good feelings into anger, and produce a desire to break off the relationship entirely. All bonds are fragile, tenuous, and marked by the absence of humor and flexibility. They can dissolve overnight.

AUTHENTIC LIBERATION

The completely nonsexist, gentle man and the strong but nurturing and nonmanipulative woman are probably defensive, crazymaking imposters. In the short period of time since people have become aware of sexist issues and begun the painful, complex work of breaking through deeply rooted patterns and responses, the growth progress in everyone is erratic at best, with regular periods of regression following any positive changes. Genuine growth is slow, threatening, and often resisted.

The authentic transitional person is inevitably inconsistent, wavering between traditional responses and genuine change. In the process. the surfacing of anger, fear, and distrust in regard to the opposite sex is natural and genuine. The man who pretends no such anger and is consistently sensitive and nonsexist, and the woman who denies any feelings of helplessness or dependency on men, have only added on another layer of crazymaking repression, or simply are skillful manipulators of liberation images.

Resistance and ambivalence are therefore signs of authenticity. Few of us have had the kind of healthy, nonsexist upbringing needed for a smooth transition into gender-free consciousness. In fact, those who are authentically least sexist are probably those who have made no great effort to be so and are not even aware of the issues involved. Their attitude has simply emerged from a healthy upbringing that kept gender strictures to a minimum.

The raging woman who makes a ceremonial display of her autonomy and the gentle man who loudly telegraphs his sensitivity are both to be distrusted. Genuine change is a struggle and acting as if one has been transformed has as much to do with reality as television doctoring has to do with medicine. Authentic transition to liberation is raw, confusing, and tentative, but does not result in a total lack of intimacy with the opposite sex.

Dealing with the ambivalence, confusion, inconsistencies, and discomfort of this change requires, first and foremost, an acknowledgment of resistances and contradictions and an acceptance of one's limitations. Women will continue to want to be taken care of somewhat for some time, while men will have difficulty with emotional expression and will fear giving up control. This is not a liberation crime.

Authentic liberation will be recognized by its *being*, not by the *doing* of controlled, "perfectly nonsexist" acts. That is, the genuinely liberated man will generate a human atmosphere, while the liberated female will create a dynamic one that invites a strong person-to-person response, without defensiveness or intimidation or intellectualization. They will create an atmosphere that is positive and supportive, not cautious, self-conscious, or fraught with fear over saying or doing something sexist. Real change will probably be as subtle and imperceptible as the growth of a plant, rather than resulting from an obsessive hammering away at issues. The flowering will be known through its impact, which will be humanizing and comfortably egalitarian.

7   Assertion Training for Women, Passivity Training for Men

REBALANCING THE RELATIONSHIP

THE CAPACITY TO CHOOSE a partner based on objective reality, rather than on the romantic distortions that inevitably lead to anger and disappointment, is crucial to the evolution of a new man-woman relationship. To make such a conscious choice, one must work through the defensive needs stemming from masculine and feminine repression. The absence of such gender defensiveness will make it possible to choose a partner motivated principally by the delight of being together. Until this becomes possible, the potential for a new man-woman relationship is illusionary, an intellectual vision abstractly attractive but impossible to transform into a living reality.

Rebalancing the man-women relationship requires

awareness that the actions of one partner depend on
a counterpart response in the other partner. The
surest way to combat sexism in another, therefore,
is to alter the behavior in oneself that allows for the
other person's sexist behavior. *In that sense, sexism
can be seen as an effect or symptom rather than a
cause, and the sexist is the ultimate victim of his or
her own behavior, as he or she repeatedly experiences the same patterns and breakdown points in
relationsips. The dominating, independent, sexually driven male comes to be hated or paralyzed by
guilt and ends up isolated and lonely, feeling unknown and sexually fearful. Likewise, the feminine
woman who is attracted to "strong, sexual, successful" men will come to feel controlled, used, neglected,
angry, victimized, and embittered.*

When sexism is moralized away or forcibly stifled,
change is coming through repression stemming from
guilt or shame or intimidation. It is not growth, and
in the long run will only create a more destructive
and less manageable relationship.

"Assertion training for women, passivity training
for men" is a label for all the processes involved in
the growth of men and women into fully expressive,
nondefensive people capable of participating in a
balanced person-to-person relationship free of the
repressed rage, unpredictable explosiveness, and
other symptoms of the traditional, polarized relationship.

Women's liberation and the relatively weaker phenomenon of men's liberation have projected somewhat distorted images of the meaning of and necessity
for these changes and, consequently, have not attracted the kind of support they might otherwise
have. A critical reason for disillusionment with both

liberation movements is the false and naïve notion that liberation or growth is primarily a matter of change in attitude, that a new vision can be achieved rapidly simply by an act of goodwill and openness to seeing the truth about sexism. As a result, the first flush of excitement is, for many, followed by backsliding. Then, in moods of discouragement, despair, or anxiety, the conclusion is drawn that men and women will always be as they are, and so "liberation doesn't work."

The job of creating authentic and rooted changes in women and men involves the painstaking, elusive business of personal growth. This will mean reintegrating and developing formerly disowned, defensively repressed parts of oneself. It is the psychologically complex, lifelong process of breaking through deeply rooted, rigid responses and patterns. Simply reacting intellectually against one's deeply ingrained patterns by developing a new attitude will only defensively encapsulate a person in another way, and more permanently than ever.

Writer Carolyn G. Heilbrun expressed it this way: "The reinvention of womanhood . . . requires chiefly an effort to widen its boundaries and enlarge its scope. . . ."[1]

A middle-aged man, reflecting on the pace and process of change, wrote the following:

The trick for me is to allow the change to take time. We're always after the quick (therefore easy) answer. "Oh, so *that's* what has been causing me to feel so alienated, so different, so alone. Well, I'll just change these patterns." Riiiight! My particular strategic error has been to expect understanding to be equal to change. I.e., if I can just dig out *all* the reasons for the way I act, then the actions will be magically modified and I'll be an integrated person at last. For example, now that I *know* my fifteen-year marriage has been a process of turning my wife into my mother and permission giver, and the resultant resentment and rebelliousness has destroyed our sex life and sterilized our nonsexual relations, now that I know that, the problem should go away. Funny how I've been waiting for a year for the problem to go away.

Authentic growth that will allow the sexes to be more open and trusting of each other as people, and not objects for use, will require:

- Recognition of blocked and undeveloped parts of oneself and how these create the basis for certain relationship choices and inevitable problems. What we resist acknowledging and expressing in ourselves, yet demand from a partner, is a key to discovering such problem areas. Women who find themselves resisting competitive encounters, overt expressions of sexuality, or the assumption of positions of power, while they seek out and expect these capacities in the men that they are involved with, are an example.
- Recognition of the ways each of us creates, promotes, reinforces, and perpetuates certain responses in the opposite sex, often the very same ones we feel oppressed by and angry about; e.g., a man may flaunt his power symbols and then resent women for being attracted by his success.
- Recognition of the fantasy image we tend to project in order to attract, succeed with, and

control the opposite sex. This image traps us into continuing to be unreal and then disappoints our partner when he or she begins to see through it. That which we most fear exposing about ourselves to an intimate of the opposite sex for fear it will negatively affect our image as a man or woman is one major clue to the boundaries of that image.

- Recognition that expecting and demanding that others be completely nonsexist is an invitation to be manipulated. Nonsexism in a pure form can only be mimicked. When it is rapidly acquired without going through difficult growth processes or when it emerges under pressure from another, it is merely a facade.

- Recognition that change involves the slow process of working through deeply rooted patterns and defenses, without simple formulas or shortcuts to self-awareness.

- Recognition that men's and women's growth is best achieved nondefensively, cooperatively, and with goodwill, rather than through having one's "sexism" constantly pointed out and "combatted" by one's partner.

In this process of growth, each change in one partner must be met by a change in the other partner, because masculine and feminine defenses have made men and women personifications of each other's disowned sides. If the masculine man fears failure, dependency, commitment, weakness, submission, being out of control, and intimacy, it is safe to predict his feminine partner will resist and fear success, autonomy, strength, dominance, control, and being in a relationship that is "uncommitted." Both

will then look to the partner for that which they fear
or are unable to express and develop in themselves.

But one cannot dominate a partner who does not
require it and will not tolerate it. Nor can one be
dependent on a person who refuses to be leaned on.
The horny male is rapidly cooled down by an equally
sexually aggressive woman, and the helpless female
is strengthened by a male who resists taking responsibility for her.

THE SPECIFIC TASKS FOR HIM AND HER

Learning to Relate and Interact Without Blame or Guilt

As the woman recovers her power to the point
where she consciously and fully participates in the
control and direction of the relationship, and he
learns to let go of the need to control and be
responsible, there will only remain the realistic conflicts and differences experienced by any two people who are in the process of learning to be close
and to live with each other.

Blaming and feeling guilty are both symptoms of
an unbalanced relationship. In the balanced relationship, the appropriate approach is "What am I doing
to block myself and the relationship from being
what I want?" rather than "Look at what you're
doing to me."

Learning to Build a Relationship Based on Process Rather Than Symbols

The traditional relationship is based on the man's
need to validate his masculinity (and deny femininity) coupled with the woman's need to feel protected and be taken care of. Each looks for symbols

in the other that meet these needs. In the moment-to-moment being-together process, because so little is actually shared, the relationship is stagnant. It is based on "what we can do for each other," and not on how it feels to be together.

As men and women enter a relationship balanced and complete in themselves, the choice of a partner can be based on how it *feels* to be with the other person, rather than how the other person *fulfills* one's defensively rooted needs. Men and women can choose each other on a basis similar to the way they choose a best friend and companion, where the primary reason for being together is the experience itself, which is enriching, pleasurable, and stimulating.

Relationships based on symbols build resentment, boredom, and frustration because they never live up to fantasy expectations, and because the partners are never seen or related to for who they are, only for what function they serve in enhancing their partner. Such relationships can be identified by the following signs:

- The relationship works best in social situations with others around to give it meaning, and does not feel particularly good in private moments.
- In thinking about "why I love my partner," the reasons are based on function or image ("He's a good provider," "She's a pretty woman," "She's a great homemaker," "He's so sure of himself," etc.).
- The relationship is most comfortable when the partners are playing roles, e.g., mother or housewife; provider, protector, or father.
- Conversations are brief and fragmented and are made up more of passing comments and obser-

vations than of extended, in-depth discussions.
When sitting in a restaurant, they may find
their minds drifting to the conversations of those
at *other* tables.

- Good feelings are fragile and can suddenly be
transformed into an angry or vindictive explosion over a minor comment or incident.

- When together alone, they have a need for external distractions such as watching television,
eating, or drinking to fill the empty spaces of
time.

- Holiday ceremonies and rituals such as meals
at a specified time are major focal points. A late
or forgotten ritual often precipitates intense
resentment.

Learning to Fight It Out

The tráditional couple works hard at being "nice"
and avoiding arguments. When fights break out, she
feels abused and cries; he feels frustrated and
hopeless, and withdraws. He then sees her as irrational and overly sensitive. She sees him as cold and
hostile. Conflicts are never really resolved.

Learning to fight it out requires the woman's acknowledgment of aggression in herself. Feminist writers often note that legitimizing female anger was a
crucial stage in the development of an authentic
female consciousness. If one cannot possess and
acknowledge one's anger, tenderness and love will
become contaminated.

The woman's awareness of how her emotionaliz-
ing (e.g., crying) reinforces the man's perception of
her as overly fragile and irrational, along with the
man's awareness of how detaching and punishing

by withdrawing intensifies the woman's desperation, is another facet of conflict resolution.

Also crucial is acknowledgment by the man of his inner experience, and his learning to communicate frustration, hurt, pain, and disappointment without feeling self-conscious and hopeless about being heard. This complements the woman's learning to be more objective and logical in an emotion-laden confrontation. Men and women can help each other in such encounters by pointing out and encouraging an alternate response. Women can focus men on their emotions by asking them how they feel rather than what they think. A man can refuse to continue a dialogue with a woman partner who will not stay focused on the issue and who continually emotionalizes.

Finally, both need to learn to define the basic, underlying issues that are disguised by a preoccupation with petty pseudo-issues designed merely to ventilate built-up rage. This requires a willingness to be honest about who one really is, and what one really feels and needs.

LEARNING TO BALANCE IDENTITIES

Gender conditioning creates a strong tendency for a woman to give up her identity when involved with a man, and for a man to have an exaggerated sense of himself. She begins to run on empty, and he on overload. He gets bored with her passivity. She comes to see his self-absorption as offensive.

The woman's repressed self-assertion lies at the root of a number of major emotional problems. A. A. Lazarus, a noted behavioral psychologist, writes that "disturbed psychological functioning is usually intimately bound up with disturbed interpersonal relations. These disturbed interpersonal relations are often due to problems in assertion. These types of psychological disturbances almost invariably include a low self-esteem and an inadequate mastery of life situations, and often include depression, rage, apathy or withdrawal."[2]

The challenge is for women to become assertive through positive expression of themselves rather than in defensive, defiant reaction against the men in their lives.

Therapists Frances-Dee Burlin and Roberta A. Guzzetta point out that "the woman who marries ... must, sooner or later, face the realization that since childhood she has been deceived; *the situation* of marriage cannot, in itself, provide meaning for her life or validate her existence. If she is to find meaning in marriage, it will not be in the mere state itself, but rather in continually recreated moments of true "I-Thou" encounter. . . . By their very nature, I-Thou encounters demand a relationship of equals; even today few husbands and wives know how to interact in this manner and even fewer can allow themselves to risk the authenticity that encounter demands."[3]

Along with the woman's assertion training, the man needs an equivalent experience of learning to proportionately let go of himself. This involves learning that he does not always need to be right, to have the answers and solutions, and to make things happen.

In effect, letting-go training for him complements assertion training for her. Any experience that promotes male and female total expressiveness, beyond the traditional restrictions of gender, will facilitate this balancing process. He cannot be too full of himself if she does not create a vacuum for him to fill. Likewise, she cannot maintain an absence of self-definition if he refuses to plug the gap created by it.

For Him: Developing the Gentler Dimensions of His Life

For Her: Learning to Be More Aggressive

Masculine socialization being an insatiable proving process, most men are uncomfortable with activities and experiences that are softer, playful, or "unmasculine." It is still relatively rare to see men in exercise-to-music classes, studying yoga or dance, writing poetry, or indulging in activities that do not have a purpose.

Likewise, femininity produces a resistance in most women to engaging in sports competitively, with aggressive discipline. Women who try often give up after a relatively brief period of time.

Consequently, men and women are poor playmates together. He tends to be bored with her areas of interest, and to become impatient when engaging in sports with her because she resists becoming seriously and consistently competitive. Likewise, she finds his aggressive obsession with winning distasteful, and his athletic passions too pressured and grim. Indeed, machos tend to turn all games into mini-wars.

Evolution into a balanced relationship does not mean he should lose his aggressive orientation or that she should acquire one. Rather, each needs to expand, so that he can play without grimness and without transforming each experience into a test of his masculinity, while she can summon up, when appropriate, a disciplined competitiveness and serious desire to win. The ultimate solution would permit both to slide comfortably between playful interaction and aggressive competition, according to the demands of the situation.

For Him: *Learning to Focus More on Process*

For Her: *Learning to Focus More on the Goal*

Part of the defensiveness of masculinity is its goal-directed quality. Eventually, everything gets done only for a purpose, be it work, athletics, sex, or relating to people. The goal-driven male works to make money, plays to win and/or stay in shape, has sex for relief, and relates to people for what he can get from them, or out of responsibility. He becomes alienated from his inner experience, deadened to process, and fulfilled only when thinking of gaining an end. This tends to transform everything he does into a job. Others sense his closed-off attitude and stop trying to relate to him except for a specific purpose. Children turn to their mothers instead of their fathers. Wives turn to other women, and men avoid each other because their interactions tend to be grim and lacking in spontaneity.

In the all-or-nothing defensive consciousness of masculinity, the alternative to being goal directed is hedonism, dissipation, and waste. He comes to feel that he is wasting time if he lacks a concrete justification for doing something.

The transition from this mechanical orientation involves developing an appreciation of the here and now, and the realization that good feelings in the present are a significant part of what life is about and are as valuable as working toward a purpose. At the same time, men's self-destructive terror of not working, the self-hatred that accompanies being unemployed, would be lessened if the capacity to feel justified and alive by living in the moment could increase.

While women are turned off by men's compulsive goal orientation, men become exasperated with the "unrealistic" attitude of women, who do not seem to the man to be sufficiently purposeful. (While he is already preparing for retirement in his twenties, she seems sure that tomorrow will take care of itself.) Men can more comfortably let go of their goal orientation and move into here and now when women begin to focus more intently on specific goals, emphasizing process somewhat less and purpose somewhat more.

Transcending Sexual Programming

Of all the artifacts of masculine-feminine polarization, the sexual consciousness that emerges from it is one of the most damaging. Men are trapped and diminished by their mandate to perform and prove their masculinity. Women inevitably come to resent, even hate most men, because women's more repressed sexuality and concomitantly greater need for "intimacy and closeness and commitment" cause men to apparently, and sometimes actually, behave in exploitative, "perverse," and "animalistic" ways.

The rebalancing process means that women need to recover their sexual impulses, whether within the context of intimacy or not, and without any specific expectations or concern about how men will respond or are supposed to perform. Well-known feminist writer Germaine Greer won me over with her direct transparency and acceptance of unadorned sexuality. She proclaimed to a magazine, "Of course I'm promiscuous. But the word has no meaning," as she described her enjoyment in having a succession of lovers.[4] Such statements are important for their indirect message that women can be sexual within or outside the context of "love." This is the beginning of the end of an age-old dichotomy: the moral one-upmanship of women toward men in the area of sexuality, where men are the animals and women the holy madonnas.

Sexuality has traditionally been a source of power for the female. When she no longer needs this indirect instrument for feeling powerful vis-à-vis the male, recovering her sexuality will be a matter of acknowledging sexual feelings and impulses as she experiences them, rather than suppressing and denying them.

On the other hand, men need to balance their macho posturing with an honest expression of their sexual resistances and limitations, refusing to participate in the masculine nightmare of sex as an endless proving ground or a denial of homosexual impulses.

As he recognizes the meaningless, self-destructive nature of this quest, and no longer fears being labeled unmanly, the man can allow himself to experience the softer, passive, non-goal-directed side of himself. The simple pleasure of being physically close with no sexual goal will then be available to him.

Further, men need to recover their right to say no to sex when they experience resistance or lack of desire, without feeling it to be a reflection on their manliness, and to discard forever all standards of so-called normal sexual functioning. It will take time for men to undo decades of psychological poisoning by sexual-comparison statistics, and sexist definitions of "dysfunction" that put an ugly, anxiety-provoking label on men's natural responses of resistance or lack of interest.

For Him: Learning to Acknowledge Fear

For Her: Learning to Acknowledge Aggression

Part of the disease of masculinity is that because fear is equated with femininity, masculinity in its purest form is supposed to mean transcendence of fear. Because he learns that being afraid and running away equals being a sissy, the man loses a primary survival instinct: the ability to listen and respond appropriately to fear. In addition, he often becomes a victim of his own "macho-psychotic" behavior when he does self-destructive things to prove that he is not afraid, at times when nothing is at stake except his ego or image in the eyes of others.

In his relationship to the woman, the more she projects a fearful persona, the more he feels the need to be fearless and protective of her. He imagines the women to be much weaker than she is, just as he perceives himself to be stronger and less afraid than he is.

Regarding the female capacity for aggression, Dr. Margaret Mead pointed out that "when women disengage completely from their traditional role, they become more ruthless and savage than men. Men and male animals will fight to show off their prowess and to impress females. But they usually have rules to prohibit killing in these games. Now, with women and female animals there is no game. When they fight it is fierce and to the death. Women are naturally suited to kill for survival ... much more than men are."[5]

Psychology professor and former WAC Captain Gladdy Adams commented, "I studied Russian and German women in WW II, and I know the history of ancient women as warriors. There is nothing more brutal, cruel and cunning than a female in battle. Look through historical accounts from Africa to the Middle East to Southeast Asia to the American Indian—men fear women in combat."[6]

A study of Air Force female pilots reported that, overall, the similarities between the sexes greatly outweighed the differences. The study concluded that men and women behave similarly in flight training.[7]

A report of the Brookings Institution in Washington, D.C., on women and the military stated that "the army has discovered that women throw hand grenades more accurately than men and are better with small arms."[8]

As important as the woman's recovery of direct responsibility for aggression is the importance of her doing so *without* a reactive or blaming motivation. The latter is commonly present in cases of spouse killing. "He drove me to it" is her usual rationalization.

For Him: Learning to See How He Rejects Women for Being Successful and Strong

For Her: Learning to See How She Rejects Men for Being Vulnerable, Weak, or "Failures"

The unemployed man and the highly successful woman have a similar experience—they tend to become invisible and unsexy in the eyes of the opposite sex. A man displaying "weakness" and a woman displaying great strength are typically not good material for romantic fantasy.

Addiction to romance is a great inhibitor to the rebalancing process and growth of men and women. Repeatedly, men praise women with the courage to take complete responsibility for their lives, but then fall in love with the manipulative female who acts weak, dependent, and adoring. Likewise, women verbally encourage men to explore vulnerable sides of themselves and to acknowledge fear and weakness, but are drawn to the emotionally detached, invulnerable, successful, and totally self-confident male.

The romantic pairing of Ms. Feminine-Helpless and Mr. Masculine-Rescuer replays the oldest, most pervasive nightmare of male-female relationships, because it inevitably brings out the most regressive, dehumanized, and defensive sides of each. In addition to taking responsibility for changing one's own false and defensive posturing, recognition of how the sexes reinforce these most damaging "gender games" in each other is a critical element in the man-woman growth process. As men and women regain their ability to be fully human and expressive, vulnerability to romantic fantasies about the woman's helplessness and the man's strength will dissipate since neither will need the other for those reasons.

Learning to Balance Intimacy and Distance

She craves intimacy and commitment in direct proportion to his fear of and resistance to it. The more detached he is, the more urgently she pursues closeness and commitment. He experiences her then as engulfing. She in turn experiences him as uncaring, unfeeling, and rejecting. This rhythm is directly reflected in their sexual experience. To him, sexual excitement is related to challenge and unavailability. For her, it is related to intimacy and love, or as a form of barter or manipulation to draw him closer. The more he experiences her as engulfing, the less sexual he feels. The more uncommitted and uninvolved he is emotionally, the more she tends to lose interest.

Both of their experiences are distorted by the filters of their defenses. Indeed, he denies dependency but ultimately proves to be more dependent on her than she is on him. She clings but later when the marriage ends discovers she likes being autonomous and in charge. Unfortunately, often neither finds that out until it is too late and the relationship has collapsed. Then he discovers a well of emotion, fear, confusion, and sexual anxiety he never knew he felt, as she emerges in touch with a detachment, rage, steadfast sense of self, and lust that she had denied. *The romantic beginning is polarized with love in one way; the deteriorated end point is polarized with rage in the opposite way.* The tragedy of the past was this either-or phenomenon. A woman could only love a man taking a certain kind of role complementing her own. *Romance was based on imbalance and thus the seeds of destruction of the relationship were sown at its high-energy, high-fantasy inception.*

Her emerging autonomous strength will cause her to need commitment and attachment in the old feminine way less; while his developing humanness will make him less fearful of a genuine, humanly vulnerable way of coming close. The cycle of feminine frustration over "It's not enough" and the masculine resistance stemming from "It's too much" will be broken to the extent that he has recovered his human side, and she her power side, and the attraction between them is based on their individual wholeness and objective liking for each other. The game of mutual manipulation can be ended. The past choice he had to make between being engulfed or isolated, and her choice of being either controlled or abandoned can be transformed into a relationship between two people coming together in a balanced way.

Recognizing, Accepting, and Utilizing One's Anger

Much of the male-female relationship breakdown stems from misplaced anger and mutual blaming. She sees him as an exploiter and debaser, the origin of her problems. He sees her as a manipulator and blamer, an irresponsible demanding child who wants to have everything her way. Indeed, many women have derived much of their growth energy from blaming men. Their changes begin from a reactive, angry attitude of "He won't hold me down anymore." Likewise, men become increasingly resentful at the no-win situations they find themselves in, and begin to disconnect angrily from women.

Mutual blaming is temporarily gratifying because it provides a target for rage release, and provides one with a martyred self-righteousness. However, there is the long-run price of ever greater alienation between the sexes.

An authentic liberation consciousness can only come when men and women both recognize themselves to be victims of a psychological process that has destroyed critical parts of them, and for which no one is really to blame. What the sexes did to each other, they largely did automatically and in the context of a learned belief about how they were supposed to act in order to be masculine and feminine.

Men can learn about the effect of women's socialization by reading women's literature and listening to what they say about their experience, just as women can learn about men. Then they will understand how the cries of hurt and anger on both sides reflect their separate gender-conditioning experiences.

At that point, men and women can redirect their angry energies in the service of the complex, painstaking, yet truly liberating process of becoming whole, rather than toward the futile exercise of defining blame and withdrawing from each other. As the liberating results of these efforts emerge, the phenomenon of feeling victimized will disappear.

Breaking Through the Actor-Reactor Imbalance

The seeds of female rage toward the male, and male guilt and suppressed rage toward the female, are contained and nourished within the actor-reactor rhythm. The degree of rage and guilt is related to the degree of this actor-reactor polarization. The best of intentions to love and communicate, and the highest qualities of humanness and caring within the couple relationship will be steadily undermined by this imbalance. Inevitably, the female reactor will feel controlled, with her identity annihilated, while the male will feel oppressed by unending responsibility and the sense of never being able to let go of his vigilance.

The change between them must be in their moment-to-moment process and not in their symbolic gestures toward each other, such as the careful use of nonsexist language. Equality between the sexes is often perceived in terms of equally shared responsibilities, e.g., washing dishes, paying the bills, child care, and employment. I call this equal oppression for both. A couple may appear to be liberated on the level of who does what, while still highly traditional in the way they interact or in their actor-reactor rhythm. These are the relationships that are particularly frustrating and disillusioning for the two involved, because the relationship appears to be so equal and nonsexist and yet still produces anger, guilt, and discomfort.

True equality that avoids the rage-guilt polarization lies in the transformation of the moment-to-moment process. A couple may even seem old-fashioned in role division (e.g., she washes the dishes, he fixes the car) but actually be psychologically liberated if the flow of the interaction is balanced.

The rhythm of the interaction—who initiates and breaks off dialogues, sex, decision making, play activities—and the extent to which the relationship is free of intellectualization, blaming, and withdrawal determine its balance. By teaching little girls to only react to boys, not to initiate, or to play the game of being hard to get while expecting to be pursued, and by teaching little boys to feel responsible for the initiation and evolution of the relationship, we launch this actor-reactor process, some of whose by-products are alienation, communication breakdown, and distrust between the sexes. The woman who is comfortable asserting her identity and the man who is free of performance and proving compulsions will more readily fall into a pattern of relating that transcends the typical masculine-feminine actor-reactor rhythm. Each can be helpful to the other by pointing out tendencies to chronically assume one role or the other.

For Him: Learning Not to Fear Failure

For Her: Learning Not to Fear Success

His fear of failure is in direct proportion to his compulsive need to prove his masculinity; while the association of her femininity with repression of aggression, assertion, and autonomy produces an equivalent fear of success.

He fears failure in anything and everything he participates in, be it work, play, relationships, or sexuality. Because some failure is inevitable, self-hatred and the progressive elimination of all activities he cannot master are part of his masculine defensiveness. Likewise, because some measure of success is inevitable if she participates fully, many women eventually withdraw from most competitive or performance-oriented activities.

Her fear of success and resulting resistance to performing may cause her to validate herself with an overinvestment, often suffocating, in personal and domestic areas; while his obsessive fear of failure causes him to be a compulsive achiever and therefore to be seen as cold and uncaring at home and in intimate interaction.

It is not the male's desire for success that is destructive to him, but his terror of failure, and his compulsion to succeed or win no matter what the challenge; while her resistance to being ambitious is not so much the problem as her fear that being strong and competitive will annihilate her womanliness.

As women become more overtly powerful, they will not need to perceive men as success symbols, which will make it easier for men to release themselves from the compulsive pursuit of triumph in order to feel validated as men and attractive in the eyes of women. Likewise, as the male becomes consciously aware of his futile, destructive compulsion to avoid failure, it will become that much easier to gain release from it. Also, when the man no longer fears the woman's success as a threat to male control, and she no longer needs to please him by failing in economic, athletic, or other pursuits, she can develop a balanced pleasure in pursuing success.

Not Rationalizing Masculine-Feminine Defenses

The process of breaking down defenses is always accompanied by anxiety because unknown and repressed parts of oneself emerge. A strong tendency on both sides will therefore exist to support each other's fear and resistance to change, with an attraction to biological and genetic rationalizations. This is not to imply that there are no true male-female differences. However, masculine and feminine conditioning produce powerful artificial and *defensive* differences. These defensive differences are so deeply rooted and tenacious that they *appear* to be intrinsic, or genetically based.

Indeed, if these masculine and feminine differences are inherent, then nature has played a dirty trick on men and women, because we have been genetically programmed for alienation, despair, and failure in relationships with each other. I personally do not believe this to be the case at all, though I do acknowledge the terror of letting go of these deeply ingrained patterns in the process of growing beyond traditional defensive behavior.

For Him: Developing Relationships With Other Men

For Her: Recognizing How She Reinforces His Isolation

It is a reflection of the disease of masculine defensiveness that aggression between men validates their masculinity, while loving behavior makes them suspect as homosexuals.

The absence of intimate friendships with other men causes the man to overdepend on and drain the relationship with his woman. She initially invites this dependent attachment out of her feminine insecurity, then comes to feel resentful of and suffocated by it.

His tendency to transform the woman into a mothering figure and to seek to control her out of an unconscious terror of abandonment, along with her own feelings of engulfment by his needs and the resulting desire to escape from him, can be eliminated by his pursuit and development of same-sex friendships and her growing autonomy. Thus she will not fear his having other caring relationships.

A first step in the development of male friendships is often the acknowledgment of loss and loneliness that so many men feel when they recognize that they have no close male friends. Many have been moved to reclaim and redevelop friendships from their younger days. Others have joined men's groups. Some have simply risked reaching out, mak-

ing overtures of friendship to men they feel a kin-
ship with.

In recent years, increasing numbers of men have
begun to share their feelings of loneliness. One staff
member conducting a "Menninger Seminar for
Businessmen" commented, "Most of these men are
too busy with their careers to have really close
friends. They come here, and for the first time they
get really close to other men. It is a powerful
experience."[9]

One man described his experience of gathering
with eight others in a support group at a university:
"A deep but warmly secure feeling, ever so tiny,
began to glow inside me. It seemed like the com-
pressed warmth and security I felt all over as a little
boy who followed my father around the farm."[10]

A man who attended a "Men's Sharing Day" in
Boston summed it up as follows: "I realized some of
my thoughts, fears, feelings weren't so unique. Good
to see there are other men as confused, sensitive
and trying to figure things out as much as I am.
Glad to know that I'm not alone. . . ."[11]

Becoming Unselfconscious and Transparent

The more polarized the couple, the less real as
people they can be with each other. Her feminine
defenses are threatened by anything unmasculine in
him—even something as innocent as acting silly,
confused, frightened, or passive; and his masculine
defenses cause him to see her as "not herself" when
she violates her expected feminine character by being
strong, sexual, or aggressive.

It is a perverse irony that, in their most intimate
relationships, men and women must hide their real

selves from each other. So women pour out their frustration to therapists and lovers, while men try to bury it under work, alcohol, and so on. Two people who cannot be real with each other, on some level, must come to feel rejected by and resentful of each other ("I am loved only as long as I am what he or she wants me to be").

As men and women come together out of conscious desire rather than defensive need, they can increasingly risk being themselves, and once in a whole state will find a relationship that depends on phony role playing to be intolerable. In the process of rebalancing, couples who love each other as people will applaud and support any risk their partners take in being more spontaneously and fully themselves, no matter what that reveals.

Helping Each Other

Rebalancing is not a matter of constantly confronting one's partner over "sexism," but growing oneself so that a sexist response, coming or going, will be completely out of context. I cannot treat a woman as a sex object without making a total fool of myself if she relates to me as a fully expressive, strong person, nor can she expect macho behavior from me if I am no longer willing to assume such responsibility for performing, providing, and protecting.

The destructive aspect of "liberating" men and women has been the heavy emphasis on self-righteous one-upmanship, and mutual accusations of sexism. We have all been part of a similar socialization process and the hard work of change can only be impaired by an approach to liberation that involves a constant vigilance against and attack on the "sexist" behavior of others.

The greatest service that any person can do for a partner of the opposite sex is to focus and work on his or her own growth. This begins with asking the questions: "What am *I* doing to perpetuate gender games? How am *I* encouraging my partner to play a certain role in order to make me feel safe? How do *I* block my own growth and the growth of my partner?" This should be followed by allowing oneself to become fully human and freed of the fear of not being masculine or feminine.

8 Guidelines, Perspectives, and Orientation for the Transition

THE PROCESS OF GROWTH

SUDDEN "ENLIGHTENMENT," or an external focus on sexism issues, is initially exciting, though ultimately disillusioning, while personal growth is initially anxiety provoking and threatening, though ultimately freeing and expanding.

Sexism is the depersonalization of the opposite sex, emerging from defensive need; it is not a product of conscious malevolence. We are all sexists to the extent that we need to have the opposite sex fulfill a role or live up to an image, in order to compensate for our own gender-based needs and lack of balance or wholeness. To the extent that a man still needs to prove his masculinity and deny the opposite, and relates to the woman on this basis, he is a sexist. To the extent that a woman, on deeper levels, has not developed her autonomous power, sexuality, and capacity to define and assert herself without looking to the male, she is a sexist, even if she is making deliberate attempts to be nonsexist intellectually.

The goal is to become nonsexist as the natural result of one's growth to wholeness, which creates the ability to see someone of the opposite sex as a person, not an object to be used to compensate for the defensiveness of masculine or feminine conditioning.

Since sexism is a symptom of gender defensiveness, it essentially disappears as defenses are worked through—not for any humanistic or similarly elevated reasons, but simply because the sexism is a part of the former rigidity and defensiveness. For example, a man will not want to dominate, control, or be catered to by a woman, nor will he relate to her as a sex object, once he no longer needs to prove his masculinity, because he will come to see these attitudes as burdens that narrow his satisfaction and experience and cause him inevitably to be the target of blaming rage.

On the personal level, actions will be perceived as sexist or not, based on their *process* or *motive* rather than their content. It is not necessarily a sexist act for a man to ask a woman to sew on a button, for example, or for a man to pay for a woman's dinner. Such matters will instead be fluidly handled according to the reality of the situation and not according to rigid ideological principles. The emphasis will not be on the *what*, but on the *how* of the relationship. Personal liberation will mean the absence of gender defensiveness, rather than externally perfect nonsexist behavior.

Growth is not an either-or process in the way that being or not being a sexist is. It is an expansion process, filled with stops and starts, forward and backward motion. Traditional gender defensiveness creates a world view to which people become deeply committed. To alter it is to shake a person's deepest frame of reference, and therefore arriving at a new integration requires a slow, methodical trial-and-error approach.

As one grows, one lets go of old patterns and confronts parts of oneself that have been repressed, and for good reason. They are threatening to one's self-image and value system. Men who have been committed to defining themselves by being successful, dominant, correct, able performers, like women who have defined themselves by always being patient, selfless, "nice," unaggressive, virtuous wives and mothers, will be threatened by the exposure of their psychological underbelly, which will reveal impulses that threaten and contradict their self-image.

The fantasy of achieving growth and change quickly and with relatively little pain or threat to their self-image makes people fodder for rip-off artists and charismatic manipulators who make the promise of such dramatic transformation. When this does occur, it is not growth, but a new defensiveness. It is crucial to remember, therefore, that people resist personal change and the giving up of sexist ways, not out of malevolence or some innate sexism, but out of terror and rigidity. It is an act of bad will and stupidity to imply that a given person can change simply by deciding to, e.g., "If you *really* wanted to change, you would."

Ultimately, the problems do not stem from being born male or female, but from the defenses that make one masculine or feminine. To that extent, women who unconsciously adopt the masculine style (female machos) will have the same problems traditionally conditioned men have: emotional detachment and coldness, compulsive activity, and fear of intimacy. Likewise, men who defensively reject masculine behavior and go to the opposite extreme will experience life as feminine women do. That is, they will feel themselves to be victimized, will be phobic about competition, and will deny their aggression.

IN RELATIONSHIPS: THE TRANSITION PROCESS

1. It is most helpful to begin with the premise that, in the self-chosen, intimate man-woman relationship, we get what we need, deserve, and are ready for. Women who fear their own autonomy and aggression most will be drawn to men who seem to be very strong, fearless, and independent. Men who cannot acknowledge need will be attracted to women who have a mothering quality and seeming ability to divine and fulfill a man's unspoken, even unacknowledged needs.

Once a relationship has been established, therefore, trying to change one's partner as a way of improving it is a grandiose, futile, and arrogant quest. The best and perhaps only effective way to create change in a relationship is to change that in oneself which allows for and reinforces the partner's "offensive" behavior. Trying to change one's partner rather than focusing on one's own behavior is a form of psychological one-upmanship that allows one to maintain an illusion of wanting change while avoiding the actual risks involved in doing so.

2. Changes in oneself alter the balance of the rela-

tionship and temporarily create a crisis, until a new balance is achieved or the relationship unravels. Blaming, provoking guilt, and threats are common maneuvers designed to push the other person back to a formerly established position and to avoid change.

3. Before attempting to change a relationship, become aware of what you really want, rather than what you believe that you want. Many people see themselves as wanting more closeness or more autonomy in a relationship, but want that change to occur without jeopardizing their familiar security. A man may believe he desires more sexual assertiveness, independence, or direct and honest expressions of anger from a woman partner, and a woman may believe she wants greater expression of emotion, vulnerability, and need with less success drive in the man, but what is wanted in actuality is all of the old, safe, and known qualities, in addition to an idealized new person. This combination is often psychologically impossible.

4. The less you need the other person to be a certain way in order to reduce your own insecurities, the more easily he or she can change, because there is minimal resistance or threat from you. To help your partner change, therefore, become less dependent on his or her fulfilling a traditional sex role in order to validate you or compensate for your limitations.

5. Traditional polarized relationships are like junk food. They look good, always remain the same, and eventually poison you. A transitional relationship between a man and woman may not look as good because it is filled with the overt expression of the conflicts experienced by two people who are open with each other and are trying to achieve a satisfying,

dynamic balance—as opposed to the pseudopeace of traditional relationships, where the emphasis is on being "nice" and understanding while suppressing the negative. The transitional relationship involves a struggle between two people involved in setting boundaries, retaining their individuality along with the relationship, and sharing responsibility, decision making, control, and power. Conflict, therefore, rather than peace, becomes the norm, particularly in the initial stages of the relationship.

6. To change a relationship, focus on and change the process (the how of it) rather than the external specifics (the what of it). A balanced relationship is much less a matter of who does what than a matter of masculine-feminine nondefensiveness and of balanced interaction in all aspects of human expressiveness. The man can be the primary breadwinner while the woman mainly stays at home, and the relationship can still be liberated in its process or essence. Likewise, the woman can be a corporation president and the man a househusband, and the relationship can be very traditional or sexist in its moment-to-moment interaction pattern. As a rule, a persistent pattern of blaming and feeling guilty is the sign of a polarized sexist interaction no matter what specific, external role and chore division there is. Similarly, if the moment-to-moment process of being together is genuinely balanced, it will not matter what functions or tasks either one fulfills.

7. Do not be misled by the currently prevailing attitude that relationships can be improved simply by making efforts to have good communication, or to hear each other accurately. The less-than-sterling marital track records of mental health professionals indicate that the greatest intellectual awareness

and most skilled efforts to communicate cannot transcend the impact of a relationship imbalance. The brilliant psychiatrist and his supportive, adoring wife have the worst problems because the damaging rhythm of their interaction is disguised by their seeming understanding and psychological sophistication.

Good communication, in the constructive and facilitative sense, emerges as a natural by-product of a balanced interaction, while poor communication is the result rather than the cause of a destructive, unbalanced relationship.

8. Nonsexist interaction means that the partners are responding to and satisfying each other's *real* needs, rather than assumed needs. In addressing assumed needs you are really only validating yourself, with the *illusion* of satisfying your partner's needs.

If a man withholds his true feelings because he perceives his woman as fragile, even though she tells him she does not want such protective behavior on his part, he is behaving in a sexist way because he is serving his own needs under the pretense of being sensitive to hers. Likewise, a woman who is always at home and available for meal preparation and other services, even though her partner indicates that he'd rather feed himself whenever he's hungry and not eat at a specified time, is defensively validating and protecting herself, though she insists she is doing it all for her husband.

9. In a self-chosen relationship, there are no victims or victimizers, only the appearance of such. Trying to figure out who is doing what to whom is an unending, ultimately futile task. Rather, focus on

what you want to change and what you're doing to avoid or block that change.

Blaming your partner for your lack of freedom or independence is a psychological lie. What people are often *really* saying when they blame their lack of freedom or autonomy on their partner is that they want independence plus the security of knowing their partner will not object or take equal freedom.

10. *Examine your expectations to familiarize yourself with your chains.* Your conditioned beliefs about how things should be or should feel create much of the pain of the relationship. Most of the time these expectations are based on fantasies, rather than something actually known to be possible.

11. It is almost always a mistake to base an intimate male-female relationship on the fact that the two partners share the same philosophy of liberation or relationships. One's ideology or intellectual beliefs about relationships, particularly if strongly felt, may be the product of defensiveness and "protesting too much." People who enter into a relationship because of shared philosophies tend to relate to each other in overly self-conscious, critical, intellectualized ways, with a tendency toward oppressive seriousness, constant mutual vigilance, and accusations of hypocrisy or ideological weakness.

In summary, to improve a relationship, focus on the *being* rather than the *doing* aspects of it; the *rhythm* or *process* rather than simply the *content*. Techniques, or external how-tos, used to improve the relationship will just be transformed by its process. The greatest sex techniques in the world cannot create passion, and reversing roles will have no liberating effect if the same person still controls while the other reacts. Worse still, techniques (the what of a relationship) may drive you crazy with the feeling "*I'm doing everything right; why does it feel so wrong?*"

SPECIFICALLY FOR WOMEN

1. Growth is not attitude change, and a liberated ideology and militancy about women's rights is often a way of defensively avoiding recognition of one's own responsibility for helping to create the problem. Therefore, you will only become embittered to the point of painful frustration over making a relationship work if you don't balance your vision of egalitarianism with a focus on how your behavior may be distancing or undermining relationships, or helping to create the very patterns you detest.

2. Be aware of the tendency to confuse defensive change with the development of a balanced state of being. Genuine growth does not mean totally rejecting feminine needs and qualities such as dependency and nurturance. Rather, it involves an expansion and development of your missing power side while still maintaining the other side, so that responses to men and situations can be made fluidly and appropriately rather than automatically and defensively.

3. Remember that liberation or growth will not produce the best of all possible worlds in men—the ambitious, aggressive man who can also be sensitive, open, and vulnerable. Rather, expect that new, unpredictable patterns will emerge. The man you imagine to be "perfect" will inevitably turn out to be a manipulator of symbols rather than an authentically involved person.

4. Recognize that your conditioning as a reactor

to the male inevitably generates deep feelings of being a victim, hence powerless and blameless in terms of the problems of the relationship. This perception is alienating and prevents conflict resolution and growth. Men have played their roles as automatically as women have played theirs, and have experienced the same cultural pressures to live up to role expectations. You probably would never have attached yourself to the man if he hadn't initially lived up to those expectations, which you now object to.

5. As you make changes in the midst of an ongoing relationship, be aware of using your anger toward your partner as the basis and justification for those changes and then being further resentful because he does not seem to support you. Your partner's possible resistance to your changes may be a reaction to your unspoken or overt message of rejection and hostility, rather than to the changes themselves.

6. During your transition, be aware that you may be double-binding your partner. That is, if he changes to please you, you may lose respect for him because of his "weakness" and "desperation." If he resists changing, you'll resent him for his rigidity. *Either way he loses.*

7. Your man's possible resistance to your strivings for autonomy and power may also reflect his dependency and fear of rejection and abandonment by you, because you may be his sole intimate and reason for living. His resistance is not a willful act of oppression or chauvinism.

8. Work on clearly defining your identity and preferences. It is the best insurance possible against a man's treating you like a sex object or trying to

control you. In addition, it will prevent a build up of intense resentment toward him.

9. Learn to fight it out directly with him when you are feeling angry or hurt. Your tendency may be to withdraw and feel abused, but this response only further polarizes the relationship and makes conflict resolution and growth in the relationship even less possible.

10. As you reclaim and express your sexuality more overtly, do not feel betrayed or rejected if your lover becomes more anxious and uncomfortable sexually. Traditional male sexual aggressiveness is in part a by-product of women's inhibitions and resistance. For the male, sexual excitement is often a matter of fantasy, overcoming resistance, unavailability, and gaining validation. As these diminish, so may his sexual aggressiveness and "performance."

11. Recognize your tendency to want to "help" or change a new lover or husband to become the sensitive, vulnerable male you imagine you want. Such attempts will be resisted by him because they have a patronizing, mothering quality. He will change when motivated to do so by your own changes rather than by your alleged desire to help him.

12. Become aware of your sexist expectations of him. What and how much do you expect of him just because he's a man—sexually, economically, interpersonally, and so forth? For example, recognize your tendency to measure his worth in terms of success and status.

13. Don't choose success-driven, ambitious men and then try to change them. If you genuinely want a relationship with a man who has a capacity for intimacy, choose one who has a history of acting

that way and who shows the capacity to be intimate with you right from the start.

Likewise, don't expect to find success and power symbols together with intimacy capacity. They are seldom combined, because the psychological ingredients of either one tend to annihilate the other.

14. Many women are well along in their development and most men, once they see that women's growth does not mean rejection of them, will be pleased. Equal responsibility within the context of a loving and caring relationship is every healthy man's fantasy.

SPECIFICALLY FOR MEN

1. Liberation or growth for men is not a process that will effeminize men, nor is it a rejection of masculine attributes. Rather, it is an expansion process that will provide more options and the capacity to respond more fully, honestly, humanly, and therefore appropriately to the demands of a situation. Nevertheless, remember that the process of growth will be accompanied by feelings of anxiety, confusion, and even panic. The changes you make will involve the unleashing of parts of yourself that you have been taught to believe are womanly or feminine. Panicky feelings may come from a belief that you are losing your manliness.

2. Critical, life-preserving changes do not require social sanction. You can appropriately meet everyday social demands, yet still develop and express the human, fulfilling parts of yourself—particularly in your personal, private life. Therefore, recognize your tendency to rationalize your resistance to growth by blaming society's intolerance of change in men.

Furthermore, it is reassuring to know that growth is its own reward because it helps you to avoid stereotyped compulsive, self-destructive masculine behavior.

3. Women's growth is a godsend for men. A woman who owns her assertiveness, autonomy, aggression, and sexuality is a partner who makes the man's life more interesting, because she is not just an adoring and ultimately boring reactor to his rhythm and choices. She is a partner he needn't feel guilty toward if he is not as economically successful as he'd like, or if he should wish to quit a job that is onerous and destructive to him. She is a partner with whom a man can be honest and who is capable of negotiating conflict. She can fight on her own behalf and is not fragile or easily hurt by him. She is also a sexual partner who is going to bed with a man for *her* gratification, and *not* as a gift to him or as a form of manipulation to hold him, nor is the total burden of performance on him.

4. Remember that a man's need to prove himself is a never-ending, life-distorting shackle that will drain his energies and finally destroy him. Work on basing your relationship with a woman, like other aspects of your life, on how it feels rather than how it will validate you as a man.

5. Liberation for men is *not* an accommodation to women's demands or to their interpretation of how men should behave. Men must focus on and develop those parts of themselves that need to be expanded to enrich their own lives. Specifically, men need to define their changes based on knowledge of their own needs rather than on women's demands or definitions.

6. Macho behavior is, in the final analysis, stupid

and self-destructive—be it a fight over an insult, a motorcycle ride on the freeway without a helmet, or the never-ending need to succeed, win, dominate, and perform in everything. The male lifespan is already almost ten years shorter than that of women. Men are at present the more vulnerable sex and need to change in order to preserve their lives, if for no other reason.

7. Avoid involvement with passive, adoring, reactive, fragile "earth mothers" who think you're wonderful but don't feel good about themselves, and therefore want to fuse their identities with yours and become your helpmatewife. You will inevitably come to feel suffocated and paralyzed by manipulations of your guilt; and she will come to blame and hate you for disappointing, controlling, and negating her.

8. Reject all assumptions and expectations about your performance as a sexual partner. You are not a machine and your responses will vary as you grow as a person, constantly changing depending on what is happening inside of you and within your relationship. Recognize your sexual respose as simply a reflection of your inner state and your relationship, not as a reflection of your manliness.

9. Acknowledge, understand, and trust your resistances and fears. They are your guides and life preservers. Do not approach them as enemies to overcome or fly in the face of because it seems unmasculine to give in to them.

10. Focus increasingly on the process rather than the symbols of your relationship. Don't choose a woman as a partner simply because she makes you look good, and then struggle to make the relationship also feel good. Instead, select your woman part-

ner based on the wonderful feelings experienced in your active interaction with her.

11. Recognize that you put a woman in an impossible bind if you fail to realize how your tendency to intellectualize, withdraw from intimacy, and focus on goal-directed activities causes you to overreact and misperceive her as suffocating you or as being too demanding. There may be no way for her to relate to you comfortably when you are indirectly (or directly) communicating the message that you always want to be left alone, and to have your needs serviced only at your convenience and in a relatively impersonal way.

12. Finally, the best insurance against losing everything to a wife in a divorce or custody battle is the choice of a woman partner who delights in her own separate identity, has a history of relating to men by taking equal responsibility, does not see women as victims of men, and has created a fulfilling, autonomous life for herself prior to meeting you.

FOR RELATIONSHIPS IN TROUBLE

The chances for the improvement of a relationship in trouble, I believe, are in proportion to the extent to which the partners know and like each other objectively as people, rather than as symbols or aids to marital security.

Many traditional, polarized couples in trouble remain together more out of desperation than liking. They may protest love for each other, but are hard put to identify anything they really like about each other when they interact. When change is attempted, therefore, there is a cataclysm. Even slight alterations in this high-wire relationship reverberate powerfully and produce crises. Naturally there is a strong tendency to undermine one's own and one's partner's attempts at change, despite the alleged desire for growth.

The change process will never be effective in an atmosphere of trying to pinpoint who is responsible for the distress. Real relationship improvement will only come from individual growth. If the relationship has no tolerance for letting go of traditional behavior, it is ultimately harmful to both parties and, though the thought is painful and frightening, may be better abandoned.

In summary, sexism is its own punishment, liberation its own reward. Sex-role liberation is not a matter of principles, values, or right and wrong. It is a matter of psychological health, survival, and growth. Sexism will wither and die as the difficult process of becoming whole and balanced progresses. Then, and only then, does the foundation exist for an authentically new male-female relationship, not one that merely seems to be new because of sophisticated attitudes disguising the reality that in moment-to-moment process it is but the same old thing. Relationships will work, unquestionably, when authentic growth has occurred.

PART THREE

TRANSCENDENCE

9 Playmates

THE CAPACITY FOR becoming and being play-mates develops in inverse proportion to the degree of masculine and feminine polarization. The absence of polarization allows men and women to choose each other based on the same kind of attraction and delight that motivates the development of a "best friends" relationship, and to avoid a relationship founded on gender defenses. The insecurity and rigidity that spring from the latter make playfulness impossible.

In that sense, playfulness in a relationship is a by-product of one's development, or transcendence of gender defenses, rather than something that can be achieved merely by following a specific blueprint or a set of how-tos.

As growth beyond gender defenses takes place, it becomes increasingly possible to choose an intimate partner of the opposite sex without fixation on image. This facilitates a relationship that is free of self-censoring carefulness, self-conscious preoccupation with saying or doing the right thing, or the need to validate one's image as a "man" or a "lady." The capacity to be in a playful relationship comes from psychological growth, just as a child's development makes certain capacities possible that were not present in a more primitive developmental state.

HOW PLAYFULNESS FEELS

Have you ever spent a day with a very close friend, probably though not necessarily of the same sex, with whom you felt a special sense of ease, lack of self-consciousness, and freedom in expressing yourself? You didn't need to be careful or to censor yourself in any way for fear you might say something inappropriate, stupid, or hostile, or something that might be taken the wrong way. At no time while you were together did you consciously concern yourself with behaving the way you were "supposed to." You felt exposed and unjudged; you had the deeply satisfying and rare experience of being truly known to the other person, in the way you knew yourself, and of feeling that you really knew them.

Because you felt so accepted, cherished, and expressive, you also liked and appreciated yourself more. The negative, self-critical ruminations that ordinarily intruded on your thoughts weren't there.

It was an exchange of inner lives. Thoughts and feelings that would have ordinarily been the most threatening to express not only caused no bad feelings, but actually had an energizing effect. You appreciated, supported, and loved each other for risking the self-exposure that made you each vulnerable. When occasionally something that was said did strike a negative chord, it was talked about, resolved, and let go of.

The time passed quickly in a mixture of rambles, serious sharing, silliness, confrontations, and good-natured gibes. A key ingredient was that you both were oblivious to image concerns and there were feelings of total trust and of being truly known and accepted.

The free flow of energy between the two of you made the specific structure of the time together relatively incidental. Your interaction was the *real purpose* and fulfillment. *What* you did or *where* you went were barely of any importance. While these aspects embellished the experience, they never became the major reasons for being together and were interchangeable with other possibilities. The relationship interaction imprinted and transformed everything, so that you were not dependent on external stimulation to make you feel good.

You had no designs on each other, either. *You didn't need each other for any long-range objectives, only for each other's presence.*

During the time together, there hardly seemed to be any differentiation between work and play. The playfulness of the relationship transformed even onerous activities or chores. Cleaning up, washing dishes, shopping for groceries, taking out garbage, waiting in lines, and getting the car serviced became fodder for sharing and joking.

Spending time together could have easily been expensive if you wanted that. However, costly settings such as restaurants or clubs may have been

avoided intentionally because their formal atmosphere was intrusive, incongruous, and incompati-
ble with the personal quality of the relationship.
Expensive meals seemed wasteful because the playful relationship transformed simple food into a delightful repast.

The energy level at the end of the time together
was as high as or higher than it had been at the
beginning. The experience had been clean, devoid
of the hidden thoughts and emotions that are the
usual toxic undertow of relationships. You had glided
on the momentum of each other's energy and stream
of consciousness, and so it felt as if you could go on
being together endlessly and effortlessly. The freedom and transparency, the feelings of being known
and accepted, of being loving as well as loved, continually recharged you both. The rhythm of the relationship was much like a string of firecrackers
triggering each other into bursts of perceptions,
insights, and ideas to be shared.

It was an effortless interaction. There was no
working at anything, no trying to communicate, no
self-conscious sharing, no learning to understand
each other. Both of you felt good and complete in
yourselves and trusting, admiring, and loving of
each other. Positive and negative moments were all
part of the tapestry.

You both looked forward to the next time together
with excitement and, therefore, it required little planning or discussion about busy schedules. It was
easy to find time because you were both highly
motivated. The next meeting could be late in the
evening, early in the morning, or on a weekend.
There was always time available for getting together
because it didn't take anything away from you. In

fact, you could show up tired and probably go home refreshed.

Looking back at the time spent together, most everything you did together took on the feeling of play—even boring tasks or serious matters. The spirit, process, or feeling of your relationship transformed the content. Just as the actor-reactor process ultimately and inevitably transforms the traditional interaction and creates an undertow of rage in the reactor and guilt in the actor, the playful process brings even objectively onerous activities to a level of playfulness.

The playful relationship requires little or even no expensive "toys" or materialistic structure to make it feel good, as contrasted with role-bound, polarized relationships that generate an insatiable appetite for bigger and more elaborate "toys"—room-sized television sets, complex computer games, a boat, gourmet restaurants, on and on. Because the traditional relationship is essentially deadening in itself, there is an endless craving for something that will make it feel good and alive. Nothing really succeeds at that for more than a very short time.

It is my belief that there is an inverse relationship between materialistic craving and the capacity to be playmates in a relationship. The less good or playful a relationship feels, the more it stimulates an appetite for external distractions (including alcohol, drugs, and food). The playful relationship can be enriched by things, but is not dependent on them, and experiences no break in flow, boredom, or emptiness without them.

The polarized, traditional couple works at finding ways to make the relationship feel good and exciting. They transform play into work, the pleasurable into the serious. He takes vacations and overplans them. He makes them one more job. When he "plays" a game, such as tennis, the game is transformed into a mini-war—a grim affair in which each serve and return is a bullet, and each lost point is followed by a self-insult. The atmosphere is as serious as the man is masculine. Soon he is preoccupied with statistics, equipment, techniques, books, and clinics. The sport becomes a compulsion. It becomes hard to know if he really wants to do it because he enjoys it, or whether he simply must. He feels compelled to constantly improve.

Likewise, going to an expensive restaurant and food preparation at home become serious matters for the woman. An evening out is preceded by preoccupations with "What should I wear? I have nothing," "My hair's a mess," "I don't feel too well." The emphasis is on elaborate preparation, appropriate manners and conversation, and expectations of being shown a good time. Food preparation at home becomes a defensive expression. The kitchen is the woman's territory and her battlefield. Intrusions, requests, input, and resistance to eating may be met with a tense or angry response.

Contrast the serious date between the traditional, role-bound man and woman and the playful experience described at the start of this chapter. Everything that happens in the traditional date has a feeling of being controlled. Conversation is measured, weighty, intellectualized. There is no stream of consciousness. An offbeat, casual comment might be taken as an offense and immediately receive a hostile response ("That was nasty" or "You're really acting silly tonight"). Conversation has a staccato rhythm and requires effort. Humor, if it is part of the interchange, is in the nature of joke telling or "clever" one-line comments, not of a personally expressive variety. What you do and how good it is—the food, the film, the music, the weather—are very important to the success of the evening. You are exhausted by the end of the experience, if not much earlier, and making plans for the next get-together is a deliberate matter. In fact, it feels like you're starting from scratch each time, like you really haven't gotten to know each other any better, because indeed you haven't.

SERIOUSNESS

The animal kingdom has been described by researchers as being "populated at its lower level by serious, stoic organisms who go about their business in workmanlike fashion. With ascending biological status, there is a blossoming of song, joy, merriment, and play; and a virtual rioting in the wealth of new luxurious stimuli."[1] In effect, the absence of playfulness connotes a primitive biological status.

Polarized men and women, with their focus on work and seriousness, resemble these primitive species. According to Konrad Lorenz: "Lower species tend to get swept into the reality of the playful activity, turning what started out as play into a serious activity. That higher species are able to engage in a playful rendition of serious activity without taking the activity seriously implies that they must be able to maintain the pretense of the activity and 'distance' themselves from the behavior."[2]

Relationships between men and women in our society that have traditionally been defined as mature, responsible, or committed have always emphasized the capacity to be serious, rather than the capacity for playfulness. Courtship, for example, is described in these terms: "It's a *serious* relationship." "They're *serious* about each other." "They're not mature enough to get *serious*." "He left her because she was getting *too serious*" or "She left him because he wouldn't get *serious*."

In traditional romantic courtship, the dating pattern assumes the trappings of being serious. Indeed, how can the dressed-up, made-up, high-heeled, hairstyled, bejeweled feminine woman and the suit-and-tied, leather-shoed, coiffured and manicured, mannered, intense, protective, prodigal, gallant male possibly be playful together or really even have fun, except by *passively taking in* (eating, being entertained, shopping).

WHAT IS THE PLAYFUL RELATIONSHIP?

There is an unfortunate misconception about playfulness in the man-woman relationship. "Playful" is thought to be next of kin to "irresponsible." To want to play is supposedly to want to be a child.

Paradoxically, from a psychological perspective, it is the serious orientation or process in a relationship that is irresponsible. The serious orientation is a manifestation of repression and role playing in the name of being appropriate or loving or mature, and a general denial of inner experience that is inappropriate to one's image. It makes the interaction fragile, self-conscious, and explosive. *It is irresponsible because of the great mass of unconscious or defensively blocked inner life that throws the relationship out of conscious control. The relationship controls* the couple, who become its victim. Love is suddenly and unpredictably transformed into hostility.

Playfulness is an elusive concept because it exists in process, not in content. Anything can be play, and conversely activities that should be play are not when they are transformed by gender defensiveness into something serious. Two different people can be doing the same activity: for one, it's play; for the other; it's onerous. Playfulness is, to a large extent, a product of the absence of defensiveness, and the capacity for it develops as men and women move beyond masculine-feminine interaction to a nondefensive relationship where they are together because they want to be, rather than because they need to be.

Certain characteristics of play can be defined and doing so is useful for understanding the new male-female relationship. One of the fundamental characteristics of play is that it is not goal directed. It is engaged in for its own sake. Dr. Arthur Koestler pointed out that the more soiled an activity becomes with other motives, the less likely it is play.[3]

Psychologist Eric Plaut, in a paper titled "Play and Adaptation," described play as "a pleasurable, freely chosen, intrinsically complete, and noninstrumental activity."[4]

Psychologists K. Sylvia, J. Bruner, and P. Genova defined it similarly: "The essense of play is the dominance of means over ends."[5]

The whole person, capable of being playful and in the moment, has been termed process oriented. In her book *Sex Roles and Personal Awareness*, Dr. Barbara Lusk Forisha wrote, "Process-oriented individuals are less bound by roles in general than other people. They are less bound by their personal and cultural past. Less energy is tied up maintaining the self that has been, or in constructing the self that might be. Such individuals are more completely, honestly and authentically in the present."[6]

Dr. Mihaly Csikszentmihalyi of the University of Chicago described the experience of adult playfulness as one of "flow," which means a "merging of action and awareness, a loss of self-consciousness, and a goal of continued flowing rather than an external reward."[7]

Translated into the daily world of the new male-female relationship, one aspect of playfulness is that it is not a symbolic relationship based on defensive needs, but instead a relationship based primarily on the pleasure of being together, on *the experience itself*. It requires that the man and woman not need each other for security or defensive reasons, but choose to be together simply because they want to be. The primary reward is the flow, the energy exchange generated by the interaction.

Play as a basis for the new male-female relationship is far removed from the traditional, serious man-woman relationship, which is always instrumental and mutually exploitive. He is chosen primarily for his functions, and she for hers.

The symptoms of traditional neurosis (which also characterize the polarized relationship), such as anxiety, conflict, tension, hostile eruptions, desire to escape, psychosomatic illness, and compulsive activity, can be seen as originating in a person's deep awareness of being engulfed by the oppressiveness of seriousness, and the underlying hunger for growth, expansion, play, and getting out of the trap. Unable to do that, both men and women begin to become more self-destructive and hostile toward each other.

Yet generation after generation has glorified the work obsession as a virtue and ultimate validation. Parents transferred their play repressions to their children. They rewarded the offspring who worked hardest and took on the greatest responsibilities earliest. These children were looked on with favor as the best and most mature. Parents could be truly proud of them. These parents were extinguishing in their children the play capacity that, if maintained and expressed, would threaten to expose their own frustration and unhappiness over not being able to let go and be playful.

Men and women alike are victims of this. The cultural preoccupation with growth, as the widely heard plaint of the past ten years, is an expression of a powerful, subliminal awareness of something lost that is struggling to reemerge. I believe that to be the capacity for playfulness.

Seriousness as the dominant tone of life, in or out of a relationship, may, in an enlightened human atmosphere, be recognized as one of the major symptoms of the pathology of socialized gender defensiveness.

However, the individual's resistance and inability to become playful cannot be blamed totally on society, as some tend to do. By confusing *effect* with *cause*, one comes to blame the pressure of economics, family life, religious orientation, and social context for blocking the capacity for pleasure and play. *Playfulness is a way of perceiving, experiencing, and relating to the world, not something that has to do with society's external reality. Indeed, reality is relative to it.*

The strong motivation to acquire wealth, for example, requires the same serious defensiveness that represses playfulness. *The paradox of wealth is that the very same process that facilitates its acquisition also may destroy the capacity to enjoy it.* The person who believes he or she can buy pleasure and still play is confusing content with process. Distraction and stimulation can be purchased, but not the consciousness of play, which requires the antithesis of the defensiveness that is the driving force behind acquisition obsessions.

Playful consciousness is not nonmaterialistic or antimaterialistic. Rather, it simply keeps materialism in perspective, so that there is motivation for acquiring only enough material security to fulfill real needs and not imagined and distorted ones.

THE COMPONENTS OF THE PLAYFUL NEW MALE-FEMALE RELATIONSHIP

Intrinsic Attraction

The relationship is motivated principally by the pleasure of the other person's presence and not his or her function. This person is an end, not a means.

Mutual Knowing

Both people feel known and recognized by the other, in the way they know themselves to be. There is no sense of being on a pedestal, of being idolized, distorted, or magnified by the other person's needs.

Stream-of-Consciousness Relating

The verbal interaction flows. Conversations are personal, connected, unintellectualized, and engaged in easily and spontaneously. There is no conscious self-censorship or concern about avoiding certain

topics, being misunderstood, or saying something
that shouldn't be said.

There is no need to maintain an image and therefore there is a sense of freedom in response and
expression. This does not imply uncontrolled self-
indulgence, but rather that any self-control will be
based on voluntary restraint rather than fear of exposure of one's thoughts or feelings.

Transcendence of Gender Defensiveness

No behavior or response is repressed because of
its reflection on the masculinity of the male or the
femininty of the female. The interaction is gender
free, person to person, as between two intimates of
the same sex.

Authentic Attraction and Interaction Based on Want Rather Than Need

The decision to come together and be together is
based on the pleasure of being in each other's
presence, rather than on defensive motivations.
Sexuality, for example, becomes spontaneous experience free of feelings of responsibility, defensive
proving, and need for affirmation that one is loved
that cause it to become work and eventually a
source of fear and distress in traditional relationships.
The greater the gender polarization, the greater the
insecurity and defensive clinging, which make it
impossible to come together out of passionate desire.

The Maintenance of Separate Identities

As the fusion of identities occurs, the energy and
stimulation of being with another person is lost.
Gender defensiveness produces the kind of fusion

that results in feeling as if one is talking to oneself rather than to another person. As this happens, boundaries disappear and the capacity for flow is lost. The degree of playfulness potential is correlated with the security and strength in the definition and maintenance of separate identities. Genuine interest in each other can only exist under such conditions.

Mutual Acceptance

The capacity to know and be known is related to the absence of mutual judging and control. Conversely, the need to present an image instead of the reality of oneself grows in proportion to the fear that one will be judged.

The capacity to accept another person is also contingent on full awareness and acceptance of oneself. The more defensive one becomes in the quest to be "perfect" rather than fully real, the more critical one will be of others. As all people become more authentically human and whole, I believe, the full complexity of inner experience will be found to be similar and available for all.

Objective Love and Admiration for One's Partner

If one's partner were not one's mate, one would want him or her as a friend anyway, because one objectively loves and admires that person—in terms of aesthetics, values, intellect, and the overall delight experienced in each other's presence.

SIGNS OF THE PLAYFUL RELATIONSHIP

Energy in Each Other's Presence (the Absence of Toxic Fatigue)

The relationship increases the energy of each person rather than draining it. Typically, the repression of feelings and thoughts, plus unconscious barriers constructed to defend oneself against the toxic impact of the other person, are the destroyers of energy flow. A sign of a playful partner is a continual, reciprocal flow of energy with no feeling drained or emotionally fatigued.

Conversational Flow

The verbal interaction is easy, unselfconscious, continuous, of a stream-of-consciousness type, and ever changing. There is little self-monitoring, intellectualizing, or deliberate effort to communicate.

The Stamp of Personal Identity

Celebrations and events are continuously created and experienced according to inner feelings rather than the demands of ritual and social pressure. External structures and supports are used to facilitate and enrich, but are secondary. Holidays and special events become tools for self-expression rather than acting as mandates for creating "joyful" experiences that are unfelt.

Laughter

You know you're in the midst of a playful relationship if there is easy, spontaneous laughter, not based on jokes or "making each other laugh," but rather on a sharing of perceptions, separate visions, and individual consciousness.

Naturally Good Habits

Self-destructive, compulsive habits such as smoking, alcoholism, drug use, television addiction, and overeating can be seen as manifestations of a need to numb oneself or escape from the here and now. In a playful relationship, such compulsive habits or escapes will not be present. Instead, alcohol, drugs, and so on, to the extent that they are indulged in, will be there as conscious choices, and never as a compulsive need.

Liking Yourself

In a playful interaction you find that you really like yourself. Even things about yourself that you might at other times judge negatively are experienced with benign acceptance and good humor. In general, you feel yourself to be eminently sane, validated, and functioning optimally when you're with your partner. There is no feeling observed, evaluated, or analyzed.

In the playful relationship you do not feel an urgency to change yourself or to work on your hang-ups though you are constantly open to input and feedback. You feel appreciated for who you are; you like yourself and your desire is only to grow and learn more about yourself and thereby broaden the vistas of the relationship.

Generosity of Spirit

The result of liking oneself, being nonjudgmental, feeling good in the here and now, and experiencing energy and laughter is an atmosphere best described as generosity of spirit. Specifically, you let each other get away with the idiosyncracies and imperfections that are typically subject to attack and criticism in a nonplayful or serious interaction. You are not constantly watching each other for slip-ups in behavior or speech.

GETTING THERE: THE PATH TO THE NEW,
PLAYFUL MALE-FEMALE RELATIONSHIP

The capacity for the playful relationship involves a process of growth and is not an either-or phenomenon that can be gained in immediate how-to fashion. The following dimensions are directional signs for the growth process that makes the playful relationship possible.

From: *What* you are based on your symbols
To: *Who* you are based on how you relate

From: Intellectualizing and abstractions
To: Stream-of-consciousness, unselfconscious, unmonitored communication

From: Behavior motivated by have-tos
To: Spontaneous, freely chosen (want-to) behavior

From: Seriousness, intensity, and dutifully trying to meet expectations
To: Laughter, lightness, and self-motivation

From: Ritual (how it "should" be)
To: Creativity (how it expresses you)

From: A focus on past and future
To: Being in the present

From: Rigidity
To: Fluidity

From: Being externally programmed
To: Being internally motivated

From: Concern about gender appropriateness (Is this masculine or feminine behavior?)
To: Freedom from sex-role self-consciousness

From: Clinging dependency
To: Being together when and because you want to be

From: Being careful and self-protective
To: Being transparent

From: Security as the prime motivation for being together
To: Enhancement and enrichment as prime motivation

From: The need for external stimulation
To: Fulfillment based primarily on the experience of the relationship

These dimensions are part of a movement in relationships toward authenticity. They do not imply selfishness or "doing your own thing," but rather a consciousness designed to avoid the buildup of repression, resentment and rigidity.

The liberated relationship of the future will not succeed, nor should it, if it is humorless, mutually judgmental, intellectualized, polemic, perfectionistic, critical, and toxic.

I like the way Dr. Michael Novak, distinguished professor of religion at Syracuse University, expresses it: "Play, not work is the end of life. . . . Play is reality. Work is diversion and escape."[8]

10   Friends and
Companions

FRIENDS IN THE NEW MALE-FEMALE RELATIONSHIP

THERE ARE TWO major dimensions of interaction that are absent from traditional relationships,
making the development of friendship between men
and women impossible, but will be present in the
new male-female relationship. The first is the capacity to fight it out fairly and successfully negotiate
conflict. This will prevent the buildup of the hidden resentments and resistances that traditionally
accumulate and then erupt in destructive and unmanageable ways.

The false standards and futile striving in traditional relationships for an absence of conflict (a
"nice," harmonious relationship) emerge from the
same distorted underpinnings that turn most of the

other expectations regarding the relationship upside
down. That is, instead of beginning with resistance
and conflict, and gradually working them through
and building to friendship, relationships begin with
a romantic explosion of "love forever," then decline
and deteriorate until finally only destructive fighting remains.

The second dimension is the presence of mutual
support for growth and change, for both the relationship and one's partner. In traditional relationships,
growth is resisted and thwarted because it represents a threat to the stability of the relationship and
the security of the other partner.

Conflict Resolution

A polarized experience of aggression in traditionally socialized men and women produces an inability to fight constructively and to thereby resolve
conflict over issues of power, separateness, imbal-
ances in responsibility, and so forth. Feminine conditioning causes the woman to deny her aggression.
She tends to blame the man for every problem and
feel victimized in proportion to this defensive denial of her aggression. Meanwhile, he has an exaggerated sense of his aggression and fears its direct
expression. He does express his anger and resistance,
however, indirectly through a critical, cold manner,
detachment, or other covert manifestations of resentment. When fights suddenly erupt, they are traumatic and draining because they quickly escalate
and become irrational, frustrating, and mean. Constructive conflict resolution constantly eludes the
traditional couple, even those with the best of
intentions. Instead of conflict being realistically

resolved, futile promises are made to "never fight again" or to "really try and understand each other from now on."

The perception of fighting as bad and destructive, and of the couple in conflict as a couple in trouble, stems from the futile, frustrating quality of traditional fights due to the prior buildup of resentment, and from the polarization that prevents the man and woman from hearing each other once a fight begins. The issues are always distorted and are disguises for the intrinsic differences between the man and the woman that make the conflict unresolvable. Real issues can only be defined and resolved once a man and woman are able to see and respond beyond their own defenses. Therefore, the same basic fights recur year after year, with increasing rage and alienation building on both sides because each believes the other to be demonstrating ill will.

Typically, couples are left to feel that they failed where other couples succeeded, and they blame their personal inadequacies: their lack of patience and consideration. They are unable to recognize how their conditioning made conflict resolution impossible and that, in fact, they are not to blame, but are victims of a crazymaking fantasy that promised love forever in a romantically rooted relationship, where actually genuine communication, and therefore friendship, is impossible even under the very best of circumstances. The loving content of every relationship is poisoned by the polarized process of the interaction and the consequent inability to solve problems, resolve fights, and negotiate conflicts.

Primary in the process of conflict resolution is awareness by both partners of the way they filter messages from each other. The breaking-through of the defenses that make it impossible for them to hear each other, and thus make conflict such a painful experience, is the very foundation of the successful fighting that can lead to real friendship.

A twenty-six-year-old accountant and his twenty-five-year-old office-manager wife found themselves drowning in increasingly more painful fights when they came to see me for counseling. Ostensibly, the issues were cleanliness in the house, balancing the checkbook, whom to socialize with, and sexual monotony. However, the *real* problem was that conflict was unresolvable because they couldn't hear each other due to gender polarization. He was typically masculine in his defensiveness. As a result, in every disagreement he overpowered her, was critical and loud, overintellectualized, analyzed everything, had a know-it-all attitude, never doubted he was right, and impatiently wanted rapid resolutions. She, meanwhile, tended to feel overwhelmed and frightened of him, was self-abnegating, felt unable to defend herself or to tell him to quiet down, cried and became unduly emotional, and saw herself as stupid in comparison to him.

Once they recognized the deeply rooted differences that caused them to grate against each other despite their best intentions, they began the hard work of rebalancing. This had to take place before they could hear each other and fight constructively, because successful resolution of conflict between a man and a woman depends on the capacity of each to respond to the issues without the distortions produced by their gender filters and defensiveness.

Before they could genuinely resolve conflict, therefore, he had to become comfortable with and learn to articulate his emotions. She had to recog-

nize her tendency toward tearful, excessive emotion-
alizing and learn to respond more objectively. He
had to acknowledge the fear and vulnerability that
lurked behind his overpowering style. She had to
own the strength and power that she displayed ev-
erywhere in her world except with him, and to see
that he was not as independent, uncaring, and powerful as she had made him out to be. She had to fully
integrate the realization that she could survive without him and that he couldn't control her unless she
allowed him to. He had to be softened by the realization of how much he really needed and loved her.
She had to see how her demand for closeness drove
him away, while he had to see how his detachment
caused her to cling out of insecurity. He had to
recognize and halt his paternalistically critical
remarks. She had to recognize her tendency to negate
her own high degree of intelligence and to see him
as all knowing. She had to learn to defend herself
against his critical intrusions. He had to learn how
his unaffectionate, nonsensual manner made her the
frigid woman he claimed she was, while she had to
work through the fear of sexuality that made her
tense and self-conscious in bed. He had to become
less activity driven and to give in more to his quiet,
soft side and his passive inclinations. She had to
overcome her great fear of competition and aggression,
learning to assert her ideas confidently, while he
had to learn that he was not responsible for her and
not always right. Genuine, lasting conflict resolution could only be accomplished in proportion to
their individual capacities to fight it out as two
balanced people, in all of these areas.

The capacity to develop a friendship by articulating, managing, and resolving conflict, for the male,

requires an absence of defensive aggression—the need to always be right and the tendency to view issues in black-and-white terms. For the female, it is necessary to directly experience and own her autonomous aggression, including her power strivings, so that she no longer perceives herself as a victim and morally superior, and rids herself of the destructive and erroneous equation between being "nice" and being constructive and feminine.

Once that is achieved, conflict will be recognized as a constructive, inevitable, and necessary part of the development of an authentic friendship. The striving to be nice and to make peace will be unnecessary once the process of resolving conflict is altered so that it is no longer experienced and engaged in destructively. Therefore, in the new male-female relationship, conflict will be seen as a necessary, helpful process for creating authentic intimacy, because it generates genuine, mutual knowing and a clarification of issues. Efforts to deny resistances, anger, and differences will be seen as destructive. The repressed feelings create a dangerous undertow, and are factors in the development of psychosomatic and psychological illness, as well as the contamination of the interaction with indirect manifestations of aggression.

It is the nice, peaceful couple that denies aggression and fears fighting that is the couple in trouble, rather than the couple that freely engages in equal, direct, give-and-take encounters when conflict arises.

The key indicator of a new process in resolving conflict will be the absence of painful, round-robin accusations. Instead, fights will be about genuine issues and differences and they will be resolvable with goodwill. Both partners will be able to hear each other objectively and empathically and will not, therefore, distort the problem or overreact. Feelings of guilt and victimization will not be present and fighting will not be seen as a hurtful process to be avoided, but as one that generates greater intimacy and friendship.

New male-female relationships, in the beginning stages, will be replete with conflicts over decision making, control, money, social issues, responsibility allocation, and the existence of other intimate relationships, but will steadily progress to a calmer state as conflicts are worked through and the partners get to know each other as separate people. These relationships will begin with considerable conflict because of an honest acknowledgment of differences, and will progress steadily toward a more comfortable, harmonious state, rather than beginning without conflict in a romantic high and ending in an atmosphere of irreconcilable differences.

His aggression will not be exaggerated and hers will not be denied. Therefore, fights will not be avenues for discharging accumulated rage, but will be over genuine issues.

In the new male-female relationship, there will be no desire to win for its own sake or justify oneself. Rather than vindication, the goal will be the genuine resolution of difference. Both partners will be sensitive to the objective facts as well as the less rational emotional nuances.

How to Recognize a Constructive Fight in the New Male-Female Relationship

The ways couples fight are as varied and personal as their lovemaking styles, and will evolve and change as the new male-female relationship becomes more intimate. The process of conflict resolution will involve a clear definition of issues, hearing each other accurately, and providing feedback to ensure that the other person's thoughts and feelings were correctly heard.

The friendship-generating process of conflict resolution will be characterized by the following:

- *Bonding*: The end of a fight will be accompanied by a greater sense of intimacy and closeness than before.
- *Nondefensiveness*: The fight itself will be free of any attempt to define who is at fault or who is more responsible. Blaming and feeling guilty will not be present. Instead, the emphasis will be on resolving the issue and taking responsibility for one's share in maintaining the problem.
- *Reason and emotion combined*: The fight will be neither a battle of logic nor a great emotional display. Rather, it will be characterized by empathic objectivity.
- *Nonrepetition*: The issues fought about will have a new and fresh sound and will not be a replay of previous, identical fights nor even a variation on familiar old themes.
- *Absence of intimidation*: Neither person will be afraid of the other, nor will they create an artificial crisis or threaten to end the relationship, in the middle of a fight. Both partners will be clear, open, strong, flexible, and supportive.
- *Authentic issues*: Fights will have a satisfying feeling because they will be focused on genuine, identifiable issues and differences. They will not be personal attacks or "straw man" fights that disguise deeper conflict.

- *A sense of being more fully known:* Each partner will have the satisfying experience of feeling more known and real to the other after the fight.
- *Closure:* The end of a fight will be characterized by a clean feeling in which both partners feel heard and the problem is successfully worked through.

The following fight between a man and woman who have conflicting time senses, the man displaying a compulsive need to be on time or early and his wife a tendency to procrastinate, illustrates the new male-female orientation toward conflict resolution. Neither withdraws, blames, or tries to use the other's guilt. Rather, there is a genuine struggle to hear and to be heard, and a balanced give-and-take that has a tone of goodwill.

CHRIS: It drives me crazy always having to wait for you when we're supposed to go out somewhere. I get so angry, I feel like telling you to go by yourself whenever you damn please, and I'll just meet you there.

DIANE: I know I like to go places at the last minute, but I'm never really late. Notice that whenever we do leave at your time—whether we're going to the airport, an appointment, or someone's house—we always get there ridiculously early. We don't always have to be at the airport an hour early, or be the first ones at a party.

CHRIS: I know I have a hang-up about coming early, so just tell me when you think I'm being too compulsive about that, and I'll

CHRIS: work on it. But tell me when you'll be ready and stick to it, so I don't have to wonder whether you've forgotten what time we have to be there.

DIANE: All right, but please don't hold it inside either, like you do—checking your watch every ten minutes, and then suddenly yelling at me when I don't even know that you're ready to go. And please don't analyze me and accuse me of hidden motives—of trying to sabotage you in some way or gaining power or secretly saying, "Screw you." It's your problem as much as mine. If I'm procrastinating, I really don't know it and I'm not "getting back" at you. I've always been casual about time. I don't like being late when I am.

CHRIS: Okay, and please don't call me a neurotic for wanting to get somewhere a little early. Lots of times it was a good thing we left early because of some freeway tie-up. If nothing else, leaving early means we can have a relaxing drive to where we're going without feeling rushed or watching the clock.

DIANE: You're right about it's being more relaxing. If you won't insist on leaving *way* ahead of time and claiming it's my problem, I'll hurry up more.

CHRIS: I do realize I'm a bit of a nut about being early and I get ridiculous about it sometimes. I guess it's part of my feeling so responsible for everything. It doesn't have anything

to do with you because you've been very
good about carrying an equal share of the
load. I'll try to get looser about that—or if
it's something really important, I'll just leave
on my own and satisfy my urgency, and
you can come later on your own whenever
you want.

DIANE: I don't love that solution, but it is a lot
better than having you worried and stand-
ing over me. I'll also work on letting you
know more specifically how long it'll take
me to get ready, and when I'll be ready to
go—and I'll stick to that.

Growth Support

It is not malevolence but fear and dependency
based on one's own defensive needs that cause one
partner to block the growth of the other. The fear
exists in direct proportion to the defensive clinging
in the relationship. It includes a strong tendency to
block one's own growth and blame it on one's
partner.

It is a stark reflection on the desperate nature of
traditional dependency that a murderous urge is
often felt because neither person is willing or able
to leave a relationship in spite of feeling trapped.
A man may be more accepting of his wife's malig-
nant tumor than her stifled desire for autonomy,
which may have been an unconscious factor in the
development of her illness. Likewise, she may welcome his heart attack or alcoholism in preference to
his working half-time, dropping out completely, or
satisfying his hunger for more freedom or other
relationships.

Growth support occurs indirectly, not by "helping" one's partner, but by focusing on one's own blocked or undeveloped areas that are indirectly retarding the relationship. You can help a partner most by honestly pursuing your own development toward a balanced, fully expressive, fulfilled state. When each partner becomes less defensive and is in the relationship for intrinsic reasons, not for instrumental ones, growth will be sought and embraced as vital to the health of the relationship and the two people in it.

The less fearful of her power and autonomy a woman is, the more capable she is of supporting a man's growth in ways that are good for him and the relationship, because he can be freed up to be a more related, playful person. The less he has a need for control and masculine validation, the more he will have the capacity to welcome her development as an autonomous, separately defined person. It makes her a more interesting, open, nonmanipulative, challenging partner, capable of relating honestly to the relationship and resolving conflict with him in a healthy way, thereby freeing him up as well. Thus, growth generates a genuine excitement and vitality that facilitates continual freshness, because each person and the relationship are in the process of constant transformation.

If growth is not consciously facilitated, it forces itself into the relationship in traumatic ways, through nervous breakdowns, serious illnesses, destructive affairs, or other emotionally "expressive" eruptions, all of which are designed to provide the breathing space that the couple has been unable to create consciously, yet needs in order to survive.

*How to Distinguish Authentic Support From
Pseudo-support*

A man indicates his desire to resume old friendships.

AUTHENTIC SUPPORT: She says, "I notice you've been
lonely since you stopped seeing your old friends
and you've become too dependent on me. I think
it's a terrific idea for you to do that, and I'll also like
you much better, I'm sure, because I won't feel like
you're clinging to me."

PSEUDO-SUPPORT: She says, "Most of the guys you
knew before seem too boring to waste your time on.
You're too intelligent and creative for them. You
don't really need them."

A woman tells her husband she wants to join a
woman's consciousness-raising group and also begin therapy.

AUTHENTIC SUPPORT: He says, "Anything you do to
make yourself stronger and more self-confident is
going to make you that much more attractive to
me."

PSEUDO-SUPPORT: He says, "I think you're terrific just
the way you are. Most therapists just make you
crazier. You ought to be a therapist yourself. You've
read so much psychology and are so aware. And
most of those women in the groups are just frustrated man-haters. You're not at all like that."

A man is not having erections the way he used to
and he's worried.

AUTHENTIC SUPPORT: She says, "I don't think I've
been very honest with you about how I've been
feeling about our lovemaking lately. I've felt inhibited and preoccupied, and I've been faking desire. I

think this is a problem for both of us and we ought to discuss it."

PSEUDO-SUPPORT: She says, "Don't worry. You'll do better next time," or "Maybe you're just too tired," or "Just relax and everything will be all right," or "It really doesn't bother me whether you have an erection or not."

A woman says she'd like to go back to school and also get a part-time job.

AUTHENTIC SUPPORT: He says, "Maybe then I can work less and stay home with the children. I think you need to find something you love to do or else life will be unfulfilling and you'll be difficult to be around."

PSEUDO-SUPPORT: He says, "If it's more money you need, I'll give it to you. School is a hassle and so is work. Why pressure yourself if you don't have to?"

A man decides to drastically alter his diet and stop eating three meals a day and rich foods.

AUTHENTIC SUPPORT: She says, "I'd like to read the book that influenced you. I think I need to treat my body better too. Maybe we can change our diets together. I've heard enough about the effects of nutrition on health so that I really think I need to learn more also."

PSEUDO-SUPPORT: She says, "I heard on a news report that dramatic diet changes are very bad. You seem very healthy to me. Why be an extremist? If you want, I'll cook more vegetables for you. We can't eat separately; it would get too complicated. Besides, enjoy! Remember, you only live once!"

A woman tells her husband she'd like to take a separate vacation.

AUTHENTIC SUPPORT: He says, "It's scary for me to

think you might meet somebody else or find out you can have a great time without me, but I need to get used to that possibility, and to learn to do more by myself also."

Pseudo-support: He says, "It's dangerous for a woman to travel alone. Personally, I don't mind, but I'd worry too much about you."

In genuine growth support, the emphasis is on recognizing and supporting the other person's need for change, and acknowledging one's share of the responsibility for creating and maintaining the distress that exists. This goes with awareness that growth for one, though initially threatening, facilitates growth for both; and that movement toward true friendship is based on the strength, expressiveness, and authenticity of both, rather than the false security that comes from keeping the relationship structure the same.

COMPANIONS IN THE NEW MALE-FEMALE RELATIONSHIP

Becoming companions in the new male-female relationship will involve two basic dimensions: first, objective attraction to the content or reality of the other person's being, and second, a balanced interaction and communication process.

Objective Attraction to Each Other

As both men and women grow toward an absence of gender defensiveness, they will be able to acknowledge, develop, and integrate the parts of themselves that were almost extinguished in the process of learning to "act like a lady" or "become a gentleman," and thus they can begin to become authentic companions. This requires that they clearly define their identities, and be open and nondefensive about expanding themselves and their interests.

First and foremost, choosing a companion will require personal security in being able to meet one's own survival needs autonomously, so that the relationship choice can be made for intrinsic reasons and not utilitarian ones. This will allow the partners to provide authentic input and feedback to each other without undue fear of rejection, and to resist the insidious tendency to polarize as a result of romantic feelings.

In the new male-female relationship, choices for involvement will be based on here-and-now, objective interest in each other's worlds. The key question before establishing a bond with another will be whether one finds the other person's being stimulating and delightful. Specifically:

- Do I like this person's friends—the kind of people that surround him or her?
- Do I resonate with this person's passions and interests—taste in clothes, food, cultural and artistic choices; attitudes toward money, family, past lovers; work and sleep habits, energy level, values?
- Am I naturally drawn to his or her world?
- Am I being objective and realistic about this person?
- Am I expecting him or her to change, to act far differently with me than with others before? (A person's history in relationships is often the best clue to future behavior.)

In traditional relationships, the woman was attracted to the man for the world he would create for her, and he was attracted to her by how well she would fit into that world and adorn him in the process. In the new male-female relationship, each will be drawn to the other because of attraction to the other person's world as a supplement to his or her own.

Another key dimension of companionship will be the expectation on both sides of being nourished by the other person's world and being. Each will, therefore, eagerly look forward to participating in the other's life and will be able to become more through the other, by being introduced to new experiences, people, attitudes, and passions. Each partner will be brought to a new fullness by the other.

Other relationships will be selected on an individual rather than couple basis. Each person will have separate friends that will be shared if compatibility naturally exists, but will not be given up because one's partner dislikes or is uncomfortable with them. Other couples may be accepted as friends coincidentally for the pleasure of their company, but relationships will not be based on the need to find other couples to be with because of the threat of having friends separately. The test question for developing relationships with a couple will be "If I were a single person, would I choose these people as friends anyway?"

Each partner will also feel comfortable disclosing the wonderful times experienced when the other was not present, without fearing that he or she will feel envious or rejected or resentful for not having been included. Characteristic of authentic companionship, therefore, will be delight in each other's positive experiences even when they occur separately.

Along with that, there will be a capacity for establishing honest boundaries that will allow three worlds to exist—*his*, *hers*, and *theirs*. Traditionally, couples poisoned their relationships by trying to include each other in areas and situations where one or the other did not fit comfortably. Companionship will mean deliberate, conscious delineation of the segments of each person's world, time, friends, and activities where there is genuine desire and competence for sharing, and areas where each desires to be left alone or be with others. The relationship will not create an automatic "we" orientation. Instead, joint choices will be consciously made. Consequently, there will be no feeling of getting lost in the other person, but rather one of maintaining both a partnership and separate identities. Boredom will be readily acknowledged and used as a guideline for establishing authentic boundaries. Rather than being bored together, alternatives will be sought, either together or separately.

A Balanced Interaction Process

A major aspect of being companions will be the presence of interactive as well as passive activities that can be shared. A key criterion will be the ability to feel comfortable and to enjoy each other when no passive escapes or outlets such as television, shopping, and eating out are available. *Being able to happily engage in back-and-forth activities reflects the deepest compatibility, as a relationship that only thrives on passive experiences suggests a rigidity in which the two people are not genuinely com-*

fortable being with each other as opposed to being alongside each other.

Companions will be balanced in their ability to take responsibility for the course of an experience, able to give up control when the other person is in charge, free of the defensiveness that can make it terrifying to participate fully, and relaxed and expressive in the world of the opposite sex.

In the activities and arenas that are shared, there will be constant reciprocal input and feedback, rather than one person consistently taking major responsibility for talking, teaching, encouraging, criticizing. There will be a fluid alternation of actor and reactor behavior, with both partners able to initiate and structure conversation, decision making, sexuality, separations, and boundaries. As a result, companions will be free of the traditional guilt and resentment buildup that comes when one person feels primarily responsible and the other feels controlled or denied identity. Each also will be able to give up control without feeling controlled—able to surrender the initiative to the other person as a conscious decision, not as part of a repetitive, fixed pattern.

As companions, both will be capable of competitiveness as well as playful interaction, without fear of performing better or worse than the other person. Losing will not inordinately anger the male and winning will not be something a woman consciously or unconsciously avoids.

Companions will facilitate the balancing rather than the polarization of each other. Each will be freer and more fluid in the context of their relationship. Rather than becoming more masculine and feminine when together, companions will promote decreasing gender orientation in each other. One will feel able to be oneself as a person, beyond sex-role expectations. Neither partner will stereotype the other. Rather, there will be a feeling of being seen for *who* one *is* rather than *what* one is *supposed* to be. Activities will be engaged in and responsibilities assigned based not on sex roles but on ability and desire. Nor will either partner perceive sexism in her assuming responsibilities that are "typically female," or his doing "typically masculine" chores.

Authentic Companions Versus Pseudo-companions

Sexism will be recognized in the how of the relationship, not the what. Specifically, what a couple does together will not define their liberation or a genuine state of companionship. Jogging together no more indicates egalitarianism than the woman in the kitchen denotes sexism. *It is the unconscious, automatic responses and assignment of behavior based on gender that define sexism.*

The woman who is a superb athlete and participates on an equal level with her male partner is not a *companion* so long as she only *reacts*, takes her cues from him, does not initiate or structure the relationship, defensively observes him for signs of sexism, or refrains from interacting fully and honestly.

A recent magazine article discussed the contemporary problem of combining "love and work" for career-oriented people, and graphically illustrated pseudo- versus authentic companionship. It described the work of an "executive heart-hunter" who arranges introductions between busy career-oriented men and women.

This dating service arranged a meeting between a female management consultant and a European cosmetics executive. According to the writer, the woman consultant was "thrilled about her lucky draw, a European executive who has a cosmetics company, two houses in Italy, one in France, and a suite at the Regency in New York. 'It's almost a Cinderella story,' she chirps over the phone. 'On our very first date, we had iced champagne in his suite, dinner at Lutece which he ordered all in French, and then he gave me a sapphire and diamond necklace for Christmas." Her complaint was that he was a 'workaholic' who is 'a chauvinist—I'm not allowed to wear pants because he says American women should show their legs more.' "[1]

Throughout this 1980's relationship, it is still the man who is creating the action and is seen as responsible for its excitement, momentum, success, and hang-ups.

A career woman and her househusband are not companions so long as there is a consistent rhythm in which one acts and the other reacts: one feels victimized and the other guilty; one initiates conversation and lovemaking while the other is always passive.

Nor are the "liberated" couple companions if both are workaholics who have taken on macho obsessions with career and success. Like two men, this couple will experience fights over power and control because *neither* can comfortably give up any without feeling great resentment. They will starve each other emotionally in their endless battles, be the battles for control overt or disguised.

One man, after reflecting on his marriage to an equally career-obsessed wife, commented, "I don't think things are as good between us as we first told you. In fact, I'm not sure we're really in love anymore.

She never even suggests that we spend an evening together doing anything besides our work. When she wasn't working, she would want to be with me and she'd get me to take time off. Now she's got her own identity and doesn't care to shelve it to be with me."[2]

Authentic companions are fluid in their pattern of leading or following, controlling or submitting, initiating or reacting, providing input or taking criticism, entering into the other person's world or opening his or her own. So long as the woman "appreciates" the man's "letting" her make decisions, he "appreciates" her earning money and offering to contribute, he feels ultimately responsible, and she looks to him as the final decision maker, they are pseudo- rather than authentic companions.

In summary, companionship, more than anything else, will mean person-to-person interaction between the man and the woman in a relationship characterized by mutual delight in and attraction to each other's worlds, and a sharing of responsibility on all levels.

David and Jessica, married for seven years and committed to maintaining a positive, stimulating, and creative basis for a relationship, reflected on the reasons for their mutual attraction as companions when they first met. David began:

I was first attracted to the quality of Jessica's voice. It had a warm, musical feeling to it—almost as if she was singing while she was talking. I remember our first conversation and some of her humorous asides. She seemed to see the funny side of things the same way I did. I remember one funny line in particular she said just at the moment I was thinking it. Periodically, when we'd be together, she would sing to herself, just as I'm prone to do—and I remember loving the sound of her voice.

We exchanged telephone numbers, I called her the next morning. I left a message with her answering service and she called me back within a few hours. Rarely was her line busy when I called her. Even though she was lovely and charming, I never felt she used that as a way of accumulating men and having lots of them pursue her. That meant to me that she valued herself and didn't need validation from men, and that was important to me. She was often home alone doing things and she didn't seem to always need to be with somebody. I liked that too. The times when her phone was busy, it was never tied up for a long time. I had always had a hard time dealing with women who talked on the phone endlessly.

The first time I picked her up at her apartment, even though it was tiny and in a run-down building, it had a very warm and aesthetically pleasing feeling. She had photos of friends and family all over. The furniture was almost all simple, and handmade. The books on her shelf were old classics and there was poetry and fiction I'd never even heard of. When she read some of them to me I found myself listening with delight.

I was into eating simply and naturally, and I noticed bowls of fresh fruit in her kitchen and lots of salad food in her refrigerator. There were no canned foods and no meat in her house. She told me she had recently been on a ten-day fresh-fruit-juice diet and I liked that, because it was what I liked to do. Many women I'd met in the past would try to be "helpful" by telling me that living on fresh fruit juices for ten days was very dangerous. Their unimaginative ideas and their version of being "helpful" turned me off. Jessica not only seemed to understand a natural life, but had been living it before I met her. She had a healthy feeling about her and I noticed that I liked the way she smelled.

The first Saturday we dated, I picked her up in the afternoon and we went swimming. She challenged me to races in the various strokes. I beat her in the freestyle and she beat me at breaststroke and I was really delighted. I didn't feel competitive with her at all, and so I didn't feel defeated. She had a playful, happy reaction to winning that I also really liked.

Later that evening we went to hear jazz. On the way home we sang songs from the 40's and 50's together. She sang songs to me I'd never heard before, by relatively obscure artists. I remember loving her choices.

When we met my friends, and other people in social settings, I never saw her become flirtatious. I have one very handsome friend who almost can't help coming on to women I date. I noticed he didn't come on to Jessica, or if he did it was clear that she would not reciprocate, so he couldn't continue without making an ass out of himself.

We had our first fights over her tendency to be late, and to take a long time getting ready to go somewhere. When I told her how it irritated me, she didn't get defensive, but told me she'd work on it—and she did.

When she got angry at me about something I had done or been—like the selfish way I made love—I found myself feeling slightly threatened, but at the same time I didn't really feel attacked, so I was able to take it in and try to learn from it. I really felt she was expressing her frustrations and not trying to be critical of me. She was teaching me something about myself, not accusing me, and she didn't seem afraid to be direct or to hurt my feelings. I never felt that she wanted to make me feel guilty, nor did she seem to lay guilt on herself. Our confrontations did not have hidden layers to them. Our communication felt clean.

I was really deeply affected by her loving relationship with her family. She would design her own cards and mail them off to her sisters, her aunt, and her parents. She would get long letters from her father and mother, who were divorced. The letters always had lots of information and a tone of lovingness without being "parental." They really seemed to be comfortable being persons with her and not "parents." Likewise, she always shared the most personal things about herself with them. Particularly, her mother always seemed to be there for her when she was needed. There was nothing phony or smothering about her concern. Also, she was not in constant contact with her friends, but when they talked, they *really* talked, and *listened* to each other.

And her animals! She had this wonderful cat and dove in her house. They had personalities almost like people and I enjoyed playing with them. I rarely enjoy other people's animals. Also, I was attracted to her priorities. One day her cat, which she dearly loved, was ill. She stayed home from work to take it to the vet and to nurse it afterward by giving it medicines and snuggling it.

It cost her a day's pay, which I know she needed. When her father was ill, she spent quite a bit of money, which she could barely afford, on long-distance phone calls to him.

As we spent more and more time together, I found I was always learning something from her—about architecture, shorter or more interesting routes for going somewhere, how to discipline animals, books, and matters of health and psychology. It constantly pleased me to discover how much I could learn from her.

When I'd go out of town on a business trip, she never probed about what I had done in my free time. Likewise, I'd occasionally get phone calls or mail from former girlfriends when she was at my house. She never became suspicious or defensive, though she would sometimes ask me about them.

I could leave mail lying on my desk and knew she wouldn't read it—not that I was really hiding anything. It's just that I react negatively to a woman's intrusiveness, and she never made me feel intruded on. Even when she called me at work, it gave me a boost—whereas with other women, I often felt checked up on. In general, I liked the feeling of integrity and self-respect about her.

I decided I could live with her comfortably when, after spending a week at my house—a place where I easily and quickly tend to feel invaded when someone else is around for any sustained period of time—I not only didn't feel crowded but, if anything, I felt more relaxed and expansive. I was much less my usual uptight self about having everything in its place and about having lots of room for myself.

I would summarize it by saying that I felt aesthetically, intellectually, and physically attracted to and in tune with Jessica. I didn't have to close my eyes to things about her that grated on my sensibilities. Her values and way of relating to family, other people, and the world were pleasing to me and also seemed to stretch me and make me more than I was. I felt I could put up with the struggles involved in getting close and being committed because so many things were rewarding and stimulating. The price of giving up freedom was far less than the richness of being around her.

Jessica then reflected on reasons for her choice of David as a partner and companion:

I was attracted to David because he was both straight and strange at the same time. That was the way I saw myself. Different but not with any desire or need to be freaky or offensively rebellious. He could deal well with the real world and yet he seemed to have his own identity, and an individualistic style of doing things that did not seem pretentious or designed to prove anything or get attention.

He wasn't rigid about anything, even when he believed strongly in something. His favorite thing to say was "Maybe you're right," and he meant it.

He could get up real early in the morning to do things or spend most of the morning sleeping late, depending on what was going on. He didn't feel compelled to always be doing something.

He enjoyed preparing his own food, and eating

simply and with not too much variety, and yet it was his choice, not a lack of imagination. He loved his melted cheese sandwiches and his salads, even though he ate them almost every other day. He never seemed to make anything just to have something to eat. He really seemed to delight in what he was making and it was contagious. I found myself loving the foods he prepared also, and I started to eat more simply too, and felt healthier as a result.

I never felt that he was treating me in a different way because I was a woman. In fact, he seemed to react to people simply on the basis of whether he could be real with them and they with him; it didn't matter whether they were male or female, old or young. And it was always clear when he really liked people, or disliked them.

He was unpredictable in his habits. Sometimes he was tight with money. Other times he spent real freely. Usually it made sense after I asked him about it. I could talk to him about his "inconsistencies" and he didn't seem threatened. In general, knowing I could confront or talk to him about anything without damaging the relationship or hurting his ego or being misunderstood really gave me a special feeling about him. Likewise, he would often be very direct and critical with me, yet I didn't feel criticized, nor did I feel compelled to prove that I was really right. It was easy to say I was wrong when I felt that I was.

I liked his passion for his friends. He had close male buddies and they called each other all the time. When they got together, they laughed and joked a lot. When they played tennis or jogged together, I never got a sense that it was terribly important who won or ran faster. And they never talked about it afterward. They just seemed to find real pleasure in playing together. I noticed that while playing tennis, they sometimes forgot the score entirely. I like that attitude.

The first day I came along to play tennis, they immediately invited me to join in, even though I hadn't played in several years and my game would slow things down. I didn't feel patronized by them. They included me and then played their regular game while I tried to keep up. I wasn't very good in the beginning, but it never even occurred to anybody to object.

When David socialized with close friends it had an easy, natural feel. Conversations rambled, and everybody seemed interested in everybody else. He was real with them, and I felt I could be too. We'd even have fights in front of his friends, and he never resented that, or worried that they'd get the wrong idea about us.

We would swim together and race. He'd always try to win, but the times when I won, he seemed to be so happy about it. Likewise, when we'd go running or play tennis, the better either of us was, the more fun the experience was.

We'd sing together, and he always knew more lyrics than I. I loved his passion for music, because singing and playing piano were my two favorite things to do. When I'd sing to him, he would get teary-eyed. I could feel his enthusiasm and it helped me be less self-conscious.

When he had a problem with a friend, or was contemplating a big purchase, he would ask my advice—and often take it. This was important to

me—knowing I could have an impact on someone like him who always valued his independence and opinions so much.

He was often quick to lose his temper, but even
though he'd withdraw and get silent and removed,
I always felt I could reach him. Or he would
break the ice after some really hard feelings by
asking something silly like "Still sweeties?"

I liked the way he put his house together. He
seemed to be clearly defined as a person. When
we started living together, I would make suggestions about moving things around and I would
add some of my artwork alongside his, and it
usually worked well. Even though it was his place
we moved into, he didn't hold it over me. We
discussed things as if we had both taken the
house together.

More than anything else, I liked being included
in things he did and I liked including him in my
world. He'd take me to investment seminars or
extension courses in psychology. I'd introduce him
to my friends who were actors and singers and he
seemed to enjoy them and respect them for their
struggles. Some of my girlfriends are really beau-
tiful, and yet I never felt that he would threaten
me by coming on to them, even though he told
me he found some of them very attractive, and I
know they found him attractive too. If he is
flirtatious, and I'm sure he is knowing his past, I
know he does it in a way so as not to threaten
and embarrass me, and that's important to me.

Finally, I liked the way he interacted with my
family. At first he was very standoffish and
critical—but he told me he had a hard time
getting close to someone else's family because he

wasn't close to his. And yet, his observations and reactions seemed accurate. When he did start liking them, I knew it was real because it was based on the changes he and they had gone through with each other.

Overall, I'm with him because I love the feeling of his world and I also feel admired and acknowledged for my style, my way of being, and the people who are important to me in my own life.

I read recently of a group of men and women who set out on a "desert dance" together. It involved a month of rock climbing and being quietly with nature in the desert environment. "In the process, self-images were altered, sexual stereotypes shattered. The women in the group discovered that they could be physically strong and self-reliant. The men learned that they need not always be sure of themselves or without fear."[3] I like that image and also the one I use to embody the process of becoming companions, which is a group of men and women around a swimming pool at a summer resort.

In the *traditional* atmosphere, the men would be vigorously swimming, carousing, and showing off with daredevil dives; while the women would be sitting alongside the pool passively sunning themselves, doing their nails, and reading, occasionally giving approving responses to the men.

In the *transitional* atmosphere, the women would be defensively off on their own, keeping male involvement and the possibility of male intrusion or control at a safe distance, while enjoying the company of other women. The men, meanwhile, would be bewildered by the rejection and futilely trying to find ways to get back in the women's good graces.

Eventually the men would give up on making contact and withdraw.

In the *transcendent* atmosphere, both men and women would be in the swimming pool and alongside together, racing, playing, bobbing and weaving, improvising water ballet, floating, being playfully sensual as well as sexual, and periodically getting out for refreshments, talking, or just taking in the warmth of the day.

11 Lovers

THE EXPERIENCE OF sexuality in the new male-female relationship will be as varied, stimulating, spontaneous, and exciting as the relationship itself.

Like the state of playful consciousness described previously, transcendent sexuality will be found existing between lovers in various degrees. To the extent that the partners have been drawn to each other for non-gender-defensive reasons, and are therefore making a choice of a partner based on mutual delight and appreciation rather than each other's symbols, the capacity to be lovers in the new sense will appear.

The phenomenon of "great sex" in a bad or destructive relationship, or even of "bad sex" in a supposedly good relationship, will be recognized as the result of underlying nonsexual motivations—a distorted product of traditional sex-role conditioning.

Unfortunately, the excitement of sex that many have come to pursue—indeed, have become addicted to—has been artificially created, and is much like the high caused by a drug. It is the product of fantasy, reaching for forbidden fruit, working to "please" the other, overcoming challenge and rejection, gaining reassurance of being loved, sublimation of anger, and even rage toward the opposite sex. These, in turn, create a perceptual distortion of the other person. Consequently, the excitement is short-lived and object to object rather than person to person. This, while initially exciting, is inevitably followed by feelings of decreasing interest, alienation, and often even revulsion.

In addition, much of what we have learned to experience as "sexual excitement" is a matter of psychological distance. The partner whose security in a relationship is threatened will tend to feel excited. Likewise, the partner who feels smothered, engulfed, or enclosed will grow sexually indifferent to the point of becoming frigid or impotent. We can thus see the futility of trying to regenerate "excitement" via exotic techniques or sex therapy that emphasizes sensual exercises or "sexual reeducation." The problem is not ignorance but an imbalance in involvement.

In few aspects of life has the gap between fantasy and reality, as well as the destructive stifling impact of gender polarization, been greater than in lovemaking; and therefore the struggle to emerge into the new male-female sexual consciousness will be a great one.

WHAT IS A NORMAL SEX LIFE?

Because of the deeply rooted gender defenses of men and women, it is impossible to know at this point in our psychological development what "normal" sex is. First and foremost, the traditional feminine woman was conditioned to repress sexual appetites and to use her sexuality in the pursuit of security, protection, and power. The masculine man repressed much of his intimate and sensual side and developed an exaggerated sexual urgency that was used to prove his manliness, sublimate his aggression, provide an acceptable way to be close, and gain control and power. The interaction between men and women has, therefore, been too manipulative, depersonalized, and anger producing for statistics on or concepts of "normal sex" to have any meaning.

In addition, "sexual excitement" traditionally has been based on nonsexual motivations and needs. This made everyone's sex life vulnerable to sudden, unpredictable, negative change. As underlying needs and motivations changed, so did sexual desire. Therefore, even the quest for sexual excitement needs to be recognized as largely the product of a destructive addiction.

Furthermore, the question of what "normal" sex is will someday be recognized as misleading because it is an outgrowth of the false mind-body split that has caused people to think in terms of "having a sex life," rather than experiencing sex as a direct expression of themselves and their feelings in the relationship.

Traditional gender defensiveness has also created an external pressure to fit a consistent pattern of responses, to have a "regular sex life" in order to prove one's normality and validate one's relationships. Sexuality has been endowed with standards and a life of its own, rather than sexual responses being seen as body statements that express the continually changing realities and truths about the relationship and the individuals in it. Indeed, the predictable sexual pattern that many have come to believe constitutes normality is probably possible only when a depersonalized, mechanical interaction between the lovers exist.

THE "SEX-DRIVEN" MAN AND THE "SEXUALLY INHIBITED" WOMAN

To gain an objective perspective on sexuality as it will be experienced in the new male-female relationship, we need to recognize the baggage of illusions and expectations that is deeply embedded within us and consequently brought along in relationships, preventing men and women from achieving a free, nondefensive sexual consciousness.

Perhaps the most abiding and powerful sex-role myth is the one regarding sex-driven men and sexually fearful and inhibited women. Under the principle of reaction-formation defensiveness in masculinity (going to the opposite extreme in one's behavior to deny a threatening truth about oneself), it is likely that the vaunted male sex drive, just like macho heroism, is actually a defensive over-reaction, part of the man's compulsion to prove himself by denying his anxieties and resistances.

Underneath the masculine facade, there is fear, rigidity, even revulsion, plus a moralistic, puritanical attitude toward sex. Real sex, meaning person-to-person sex rather than sex with a sex object or fantasy, is intimidating and unattractive. For sex to be exciting for most men, it must be held at a distance, controlled, depersonalized, and made into a fantasy.

Because of pressures the male feels to perform "like a man," the woman can even become an aversive stimulus. That is, whenever he can't perform, she becomes a threat—a witness to his failure and a source of anxiety and fear.

Most of the elements of true sexuality are not even available to men because of the repressions that result from masculinity. The man loses much of his capacity to express feelings and needs; to be unconcerned with performance; to be passive as well as active; to be playful, sensual, and generally able to relate to the woman as the person she really is and not as a fantasy sex object. Indeed, his lovemaking capacity has been crippled and needs to be significantly redeveloped.

While women's literature on sexuality is filled with encouragement to experience, experiment, and push out the limits, contemporary sexual literature for men tends to be negative, anxiety ridden, and focused on problems, fears, and declining potency.

Indeed, the sexually and sensually more comfortable, expressive, and exploratory gender will most likely turn out to be the female. Emerging female sexuality is increasingly expansive and celebratory. Compare the rigid sexuality of men, where there is only one acceptable standard, to today's female sexual consciousness, where almost all options are considered not only acceptable, but valuable as avenues to growth.

Masturbation, for example, has been exalted by many women writers. Artist Betty Dodson, in an art show, celebrated female masturbation with a series of slides depicting the genitals of twenty women. Her book *Liberating Masturbation* was an important document of feminist consciousness. She wrote, "I now feel that masturbation is a form of meditation on self-love. When I masturbate, I create a space for myself in the very same way I would for a sepcial love—soft lights, candles, incense, music, colors, textures, sexual fantasies, anything that turns me on. If I use my hand, I also use oil or cream. The slippery, moist feeling of oil on my genitals is very sensuous."[1]

Becoming Orgasmic: A Sexual Growth Program for Women, written by three prominent psychologists, includes exercises for women such as looking at yourself, exploration by touch, relaxation exercises, vaginal exercises, touching for pleasure, using erotic literature, fantasizing, using a vibrator, sharing self-discoveries with your partner, and "pleasuring each other."[2]

Other alternatives are accepted and supported, be they sexual experiences with other women, bisexuality, involvement with more than one lover, older lovers, very young lovers, sensuality without direct sexuality, or even celibacy if a woman prefers to direct her energy elsewhere due to a lack of desire, no suitable partners, or philosophical reasons.

While men dwell on their fears, women are exploring their increasing and varied appetites. Psychiatrist Mary Jane Sherfey, in her book *The Nature and Evolution of Female Sexuality*, presents the thesis that women are by nature sexually insatiable. This insatiability has been suppressed by men through the mechanisms of civilization and more directly.[3]

Well-known sex educator Dr. Mary Calderone agrees that "The sexual potential of women is almost infinite in its variety and richness."[4]

In her study of Moroccan women, anthropologist Daisy Hilse Dwyer of Columbia University described the subordination of females, based partly on the belief that as women and men get older, women progress toward sexual depravity and men toward saintliness. It is thought that women's unharnessed sexuality would undermine social order and destroy the capacity for motherly love.[5]

BECOMING LOVERS

The beginning phases of the new male-female sexuality will be surrounded by anxiety resulting from men's and women's efforts to release themselves from the many deeply rooted false beliefs and distorted self-definitions they have been raised with regarding their sexuality. Initial attempts to change are threatening on both sides, as men must acknowledge sexual fears and fragility, and bewilderment at being unable to cope with what they thought they wanted—an overtly sexual woman; and as women more directly and *nonmanipulatively* express their strong sexuality and sensuality, thereby giving up a time-honored instrument of feminine power, along with their notions of what being feminine means. When sex is no longer a defensive proving ground for the man's masculinity, and when the woman no longer needs sex as a means of control, the experience of a real person being in bed with a real person, with no hidden, deeper motives or needs operating to color the experience, can exist. Arriving at the new male-female consciousness means, therefore, that the man will have broken through his machine-consciousness and masculine compulsions, and will no longer view his sexuality as a vehicle for proving his manliness. The woman, meanwhile, will have reclaimed power and autonomy so that she will have no defensive need to please him, to be passive, to present an appropriate image of femininity, or to feel threatened if he does not perform "like a man."

Optimal sexuality will, therefore, require that each be capable of being fluid in responses, able to be aggressive or passive, dominant or submissive, sexual or sensual or neither, without preconceptions about who should do what because of gender.

The emphasis will be placed on the process of the relationship as a way to understand the sexual experience. Sexual responses will be seen simply as expressions of the real feelings and underlying motivations of the two people involved, and it is this process that will be explored when attempting to understand a couple's experience, rather than the sexual behavior itself.

When sexuality is troubled, the relationship and its rhythm or process will be focused on. Sexual responses will be perceived simply as body statements and guides to understanding the relationship and the individuals involved. "Dysfunctional" responses will be translated into feeling language; "I don't really want to be close" or "I'm feeling responsible and pressured" may replace and redefine "impotence," and "I don't want you because I resent your control" or "I don't feel really turned on to you as a person" may replace labels such as "vaginismus." Discussion will not be about sexual problems but about the expectations and feelings of the partners in the relationship. Focusing on "problems" and their external "solutions" will be recognized as a way of evading the relationship's realities.

The anxiety-generating language of sexual dysfunction—words such as "primary" or "secondary impotence," "frigidity," and the like—will be recognized as a form of intellectualized avoidance and an insult to the integrity of the person, and will therefore not be used as a frame of reference.

Couples will not speak of a sex life as something separate from themselves, but will perceive sex simply as one true expression of the nature of their relationship. They will recognize that *they are* their sexual responses; they don't have a sexual response that exists by itself. Thus the false division between mind and body will begin to dissolve.

The focus on sexual statistics that was part of polarized sexuality, with the man proving his masculinity by meeting a rigid mechanical standard and the woman seeking to please and gain reassurance, will shift. The tyranny of numbers that purport to define normal sexuality will be recognized as destructive relics of traditional defensive compulsions, and will be rejected.

The pattern of sexual activity, once free of defensiveness, will be ever changing and unpredictable, reflecting the inner states of the separate partners and their feelings about the relationship. Sometimes, sex will be frequently engaged in, and at other times, not at all. Sometimes, just holding each other will be enough; at other times, powerful sexual desire will be there and will be acted on. Sexual rhythm will be affected by everything that affects the relationship.

A drop in sexual activity, for example, will be

looked at for the statement it is making about the relationship, and not necessarily as a sign of its deterioration. In the traditional relationship, where sex was a main reason for being together and was a service provided for the man by the woman to salve his masculinity needs, the amount of sex was of critical concern.

The new male and female partners will not seek out how-tos to "improve" their sex life, because no technique can create feeling. Techniques, in general, only promote evasion and disguise resistance, like spices on spoiled food. Using them to cope with problems will be seen as a violation of the persons involved. The question of "how to," therefore, will also be seen as a way of intellectually evading a confrontation with the personal and emotional aspects of the relationship.

In the new male-female relationship, sex will not be a foreground concern, but will be for enhancement and play. The choice of partners will be based on the feelings of playfulness the person engenders, along with his or her openness, aesthetics, values, physical attractiveness, ability to be real and to resolve conflict, and sense of true knowing and being known. Therefore, the state of one's personal development, what one comes to the relationship with, will determine the nature of the experience.

Sex in the new male-female relationship will accordingly be exciting in proportion to the energy level of real mutual feelings. Sexual experiences may not, however, have the electric, "great-sex" feeling that occurs when an experience is saturated with fantasy. I am reminded of a description of the statues on Hindu temples, which contain much overt sexual display: "The figures are sexually active, but they are not obsessed; they are at ease; they are in the world but not of it; they play";[6] the stone lovers on some temples "reveal rapture, not passion. . . . They show no urgency, but rest in serene, almost meditative poses."[7]

New male-female sexuality will be effortless, unselfconscious, and playful when engaged in honestly, as sex between two people who just want to be next to each other when they are genuinely inclined to be. The quality and ease of the experience will be dependent on the extent of feeling known, valued, safe, connected, attracted, loving and loved, bonded, and stimulated by each other's presence.

The form of the sexual relationship will be custom fitted to the needs of the partners and not superimposed on them. A desire to experiment with the structure, such as through an open marriage, will be discussed in terms of "What is it telling us about how we feel and where we are with each other?" rather than what open marriage will supposedly do for the couple.

Sexuality will no longer be a matter for obsession or even major interest. It will not be something to write books about, or develop techniques for, when it is realized that each sexual experience is unique unto itself and the relationship, and that sex is simply an ever changing expression of the consciousness or feelings of the two partners. Defensive sexuality, on the other hand, will be recognized as sex engaged in for manipulative or hostile motives, and a source of body tensions, resistances, and feelings of emptiness.

Because the new male-female relationship will be a fluid interaction between two total people, each capable of the full range of human responses, we only owe it to ourselves and our partners to develop ourselves fully. Then we will naturally come to lovemaking for no other reason than a genuine desire for closeness and sensual-sexual contact with that particular person.

THE NEW PARTNERS

Brian and Margaret are illustrative of a couple whose sexual interaction expresses their individual changes and mutual growth toward a new male-female relationship. As such, they experience sex as a direct expression of their relationship and its changes and development. Their sexuality is representative of the new male-female experience, not because it illustrates a different or spectacular sex life, but because it was accurately understood and worked through. It is rooted in the currents of their interaction, their struggle for growth, and their separate selves.

When they first met, like most couples in the initial flush of being strongly attracted and very much in love, they had sex frequently and anywhere they could. Brian was attracted to Margaret because he saw her as an independent, separate, creative, strong, and exciting person. He felt totally aroused by her—physically, emotionally, and spiritually. Margaret was drawn to Brian's sensitivity, openness, humor, intelligence, and passion for his work as an architect.

Brian initially thought that their sex was the best he'd ever experienced. He felt himself being both primitive and refined, sensitive to her yet "animalistic." Margaret loved Brian's passion and urgency, but was bothered by how quickly he always seemed to move toward intercourse. She picked up on his underlying fear of not performing well, while at the same time he never asked her whether she had had an orgasm, or if there was something that he could do for her. For two months Margaret did not confront him about this because she did not want to inhibit his spontaneity.

Both clearly had nonsexual motives operating during their sex. Margaret wanted to please and hold on to Brian. Brian wanted to make sure he projected a strong, confident image.

One evening, in an unguarded moment, Margaret became openly angry because Brian entered her and ejaculated almost immediately after they started kissing. Brian's initial reaction was one of feeling resentful, betrayed, even shocked. If she had all these feelings about his sexual "selfishness," why hadn't she told him sooner? Margaret replied that she was only now feeling confident enough to confront him. While Brian could accept this intellectually, it caused him to become inhibited and anxious to the point where his erections did not last as they had before. He blamed her: "You put a damper on my spontaneity. If I have to worry about your orgasms, how can I be natural?" He also felt jarred by the fact that he hadn't picked up on Margaret's discontent sooner.

This led to a discussion that called into question many of Brian's notions. Margaret told him that he didn't need to perform for her. She would rather he displayed more awareness of her as a person. Brian realized he wasn't as tuned in to Margaret as he thought, and that his notion of spontaneity really disguised his fear that if he stopped to think about a woman's needs, he would lose his sexual momentum and confidence. He also realized that he had been compulsively having sex with her on a regular basis to test himself, and partially to reassure her that he found her attractive, often when he didn't really want to.

This caused Brian to withdraw somewhat. He felt confused and told Margaret that he wasn't going to initiate sex for a while because he was trying to sort out his true feelings. Margaret responded that she'd enjoy initiating it, and hadn't done so in the past only because Brian was so sexually urgent all the time that there didn't seem to be an opportunity.

A period of self-consciousness followed for both. Margaret began to initiate sex and, to her dismay, Brian's response was often much less passionate than it had been before. Sometimes it would take quite some time and effort for him to get hard. Brian sensed it bothered Margaret and she acknowledged it. She recognized also the judgments she made about him for not having an erection, and how this made Brian feel criticized.

Consequently, both became more conscious of each other's reality and also more self-conscious. Even though Brian felt unsure sexually, because he thought he was losing control in the relationship, Margaret told him that her orgasms were now deeper and much more fulfilling. This was true even though Brian's erections were not as spontaneous and strong as they had been. This surprised him.

Though he felt sexually insecure, he also felt more real with Margaret and increasingly less concerned about his erections. Often now they would just cuddle in bed without having sex, and Brian enjoyed that immensely. Sometimes Margaret would become horny and aggressive, and she would bring herself, and then him, to orgasm. He felt his anxiety disappear and she no longer felt threatened by his slow response or lack of one.

The kind of thrill that was there for Brian at the beginning diminished, but was replaced by another kind of pleasure—feeling real, relaxed, and accepted. Margaret was enjoying herself more now than initially, because she experienced a sense of connection, of being cared about and "taken in" by Brian.

Their sexuality became more playful. They would talk and laugh in bed for long periods of time before beginning to have sex. Margaret was now very much a person in Brian's eyes, and vice versa, so that just jumping into bed and making love often seemed too impersonal, mechanical, and inappropriate.

When Margaret became too clinging because of her difficulties at work, and her desire to "be a little girl" came out, Brian noticed himself sexually turning off completely. They talked about it and Brian confronted her with the fact that her intense demands for closeness took away the distance he needed to appreciate her as a separate person. Likewise, Brian would periodically become jealous of Margaret when she had dinner with her male co-workers or a neighbor flirted with her. He would seek reassurance in bed and Margaret found herself unable to respond. They discussed it, and Brian realized that he didn't really want sex at such times, but proof of Margaret's loyalty.

Their sexual experiences began to take on great variability. They would have sex several days in a row, then not at all for a week or more. Sometimes, they felt intimate but not sexual. At other times, particularly during an intense period when they fully experienced their mutual delight in each other, passion dominated and sex was wonderfully exciting. Throughout, they began to see how their sexual responses toward each other reflected perfectly what was going on between them. Increasingly, sex became just one part of a total, changing, and nourishing relationship.

12 Passing the Baton: A New Parenting Consciousness

PASSING THE BATON is a metaphor for parenting at a time when the parents themselves are fully grown, whole, and ready on every level, so that becoming a parent does not subtract anything, but enhances, expands, and allows for a largely conflict-free and therefore stressless experience, and genuinely loving responses. It is less a matter of the age of the parents than of their readiness, though it is difficult to imagine any male or female becoming sufficiently aware, in the sense of having lived out major aspirations and fantasies, at the young age when most people have children. In fact, I believe that men and women who are free of gender-defensive compulsions will naturally resist parenting until they are fully ready to pass the baton.

One result of the traditional relationship is that children are usually conceived at a time when the parents themselves have barely entered their adult lives, let alone become whole and fulfilled people. It becomes a matter of "babies having babies," as parents who are still in the early stages of their own formation encumber themselves with parenting responsibilities. They are having the children at the starting gate of their lives when their race has barely begun, rather than near the finish line when having a child would be more a matter of passing the baton. Thus children become a burden for whom sacrifices have to be made. Inevitably, the love of parent for child becomes tainted by underlying resentment and ambivalence because the child represents a mixed blessing—a source of satisfaction, but also an obstacle to the parents' unrealized fantasies of freedom, pleasure, and growth.

While we are told that the reluctance on the part of many people today to have children is a reflection of a trend toward narcissism, it is the traditional parents conceiving young and automatically who are truly narcissistic. They relate to their children as extensions of themselves. Children are expected to reflect favorably on their parents' images and values—to make the parents look good and also fulfill their parents' needs—in gratitude for what they received. Often, children are even pressured to live out their parents' frustrated aspirations. In that sense, they are used by their parents—desired and related to more as symbols than as ongoing separate presences. Therefore, children often get the message that they are in the way and are resented for being there. "Children should be seen and not heard" is a classic articulation of the phenomenon of relating to the child as a symbol, while rejecting him or her as a person.

A negative cycle is created. Parents who relate to their children instrumentally, ambivalently, and guiltily ("I *should* do this for the kids") are, when their children grow up, treated by them manipulatively, ambivalently, and with heavy doses of guilt motivation. They feel angered and hurt by this seeming rejection. There is an ever widening "generation gap" as an inevitable outgrowth of the resistances, resentments, and ambivalence on both sides.

"MY PARENTS DIDN'T LOVE ME"

The feeling of failed communication between oneself and one's parents and the sense that one was not truly loved and cared for as a child are very common. Genuinely loving parenting, as opposed to narcissistic and self-serving parenting, is rare. *"My parents didn't love me,"* therefore, *is more or less everybody's story. Parents don't love their children, not because they don't want to, but simply because they are not prepared, fulfilled, or able to love them, due to their own immaturities and underlying frustrations. A significant amount of resentment of child by parent is inevitable, to the extent that the child represents an obstacle to the parents' undeveloped selves.*

For the traditional young woman, becoming a mother is primarily a way of achieving an identity. It is also a way of gaining power in a marital relationship where she feels controlled by her husband and related to like a child. Becoming a mother provides her additional security by entrenching her more firmly in the care, protection, responsibility, and therefore guilt responses of her husband. Thus, she uses her child to complete and compensate for the feminine defenses that prevent her from being a whole person.

Because the child is the major focus of her identity, she tends to destructively overmother, as her sense of value as a person depends on her being seen as a good mother. As feminist author Alice Rossi wrote, "I suspect that the things women do for and with their children have been needlessly elaborated to make motherhood a full-time job. Unfortunately, in this very process the child's struggle for autonomy and independence; for privacy and the right to worry things through for himself are subtly and pervasively reduced by the omnipresent mother."[1]

This mothering style has been termed "momism" by one psychologist, and called "the silent disease of America."[2] These are mothers who devote themselves completely to the creation of a perfect child and in so doing ensure the production of an emotional cripple.

Likewise, the child is used by the male in that becoming a father is a symbolic validation of his masculinity—something he does for his image as a man, to have an heir, and to "please" and control his wife who is now a more dependent, secure possession, rather than to participate in the active process of fathering, which he is unprepared for and resistant to. The traditional masculine discomfort with touching, holding, sensuality, emotional expression, playfulness, and non-goal-directed activity, plus his preoccupations with career, money, and manly performance, make him literally incapable of healthy, active fathering. Only recently have men begun to acknowledge and attempt to change themselves so they can become positive participants in the parenting process.

Tragically, the traditional father, with the best of intentions toward his family, is doomed to be alienated from, even hated by his own children. For one thing, his is usually the role of disciplinarian. Secondly, the more traditionally masculine he is, the more he tends to be critical, ungiving, and emotionally distant. Even when he plays the role of "nice guy" he is still frequently viewed as self-centered and insensitive. The fruits of his misplaced dedication to his family are, therefore, mere tolerance because he "means well," and perhaps some muted affection at best. More often he is remembered with resentment and bitterness.

Describing the traditional interaction of the Latin American couple, Evelyn P. Stevens has this to say about the payoff for being a macho father (italics added): "Secure in the knowledge that her imperfections are immaterial, the Latin American woman wages undeclared war on her husband. Is he stingy? The children are taught to shame him by their tearful begging. Is he abusive? The children are there to comfort their mother. Is he unfaithful? The children's admiration for their mother's abnegation only increases. Does he indulge in petty harassments? The children's silent hostility can be felt. *In sum, his efforts to sustain his reputation as a macho in the world outside of the home require that he relinquish his claims to respect and love within the home.*"[3]

One man, remembering his relationship with his father, said, "If I did it one way, I was wrong. If I did it the other way, I was wrong." Another expressed his feelings more vehemently: "I hate Dad! Nothing I ever do is good enough! Everything gets criticized. He's always insulting me and he treats

Mother like dirt." A third man expressed his rage directly, when he told his abusive, alcoholic father, "Stay out of my life. You've always been a monkey on my back." The young son of a divorced mother who was in the middle of painful divorce litigation told his mother, "Why doesn't somebody murder him? If he's your ex-husband, why can't he be my ex-father?"

When a father is threatening or even hated, the son is left with no positive male figure with whom to identify. In fact, in reaction he may attempt to become everything his father is not. It is hardly surprising that sexual-identity confusion is so common among males. Men work hard at feigning masculinity, but are often confused and frightened as to what manliness really is and feels like, partially because the father has been such a negative identification figure.

While the traditional father is a shadowy or negative presence, he is counterbalanced by the exaggerated parenting of his wife, who lives through the children. While the macho father is doomed to being disliked, the mother is seen either as a relentless, suffocating person or as a self-sacrificing saint, who puts up with so much unhappiness "she should have left Dad twenty years ago." Her children relate to her out of gratitude because of how she "sacrifices" herself and, often, they never resolve their dependency and guilt feelings toward her. Grown men and women still spend a lifetime relating to their mothers as guilt-ridden, approval-seeking, rejection-fearing children. Their mother is a child herself and as such she cannot love them, nor can they love her as a person in her own right, because she has never been such a person with them.

The unbalanced combination of the domineering, suffocating mother and the weak, passive father or the tyrannical, forbidding father and the self-sacrificing mother is most people's experience. This is the inevitable outgrowth of masculine and feminine roles and defensiveness. *No one is to blame, but everyone is damaged by the unending, destructive parenting cycle.*

The combination of the domineering, suffocating mother and the weak, passive father is lethal to the son, who is pressured to "act like a man" without actually having a strong male presence to identify with. It also harms the daughter. As sociologist Nancy Chodorow commented, "The mothers had emotional needs which weren't being met by close kin or by their husbands either. . . . It inflated the importance of their relation to their child and made it unbearably intense. The daughter's ambivalence, if not fury, is greatest in just this situation. Its cause is the role of the mother as much as, or more than the particular person she is."[4]

One woman interviewed about her relationship with her mother commented, "There's no doubt that my mother gave me a lot of grief and drove me crazy with criticism, but it wasn't all her fault. There was real pressure on her from my father to stay home and mangle us with perfect motherhood. And where the hell was he? On the 7:02 from Port Washington. He was never around. And when he was, he was like a kindly uncle, a surprise giver. It was my mother who had to be the heavy."[5]

These are the inevitable and tragic outgrowths of parenting by the child-woman, who lives through her role as a wife-mother, and the machine-male, who handles his difficulty relating as a person by withdrawing from personal involvement and turning the responsibility for the personal dimensions of life over to his wife.

It is also a pathetic, pathological manifestation of our blindness that the spiral of marrying and parenting young continues and is actually encouraged in most parts of the country, even as we get closer and closer to a collapse in parent-child and other family relationships.

A study reported by Dr. Richard J. Gelles of the University of Rhode Island, and based on the examination of 2,143 American families, found that young parents are the most violent and destructive. "The rate of abusive violence among parents 30 years old or younger, is 62 percent higher than the rate among those 31 to 50 years of age. Those 30 and under were more than 5 times more violent than individuals over 50. . . . We need to recognize that younger families require the most concentrated treatment and prevention resources if we are ever to reduce the level of family violence."[6]

Psychologist Bertran J. Cohler, based on interviews with mothers during his fifteen years of experience at various Chicago clinics and hospitals, said, "One-sixth of all young mothers suffer such severe mental depression as a result of motherhood that they require professional care. A larger, but unspecified percentage struggle with the stresses of motherhood with varying degrees of success, but are far from happy with their lot in life." He concluded that "only sudden death is as stressful as the birth of a first child and the depression, grief and mourning women undergo after giving birth is very understandable. . . . Young mothers are anchored between the heavy responsibilities of caring for their own kids and meeting the growing demands of their own parents, grandparents and husbands."[7]

Another effect of parenting at a young age was discovered in a study based on information from 2,480 married couples in an urban area. It concluded that *parenthood detracts from the physical and psychological health of husbands and wives, particularly among young couples.*[8]

THE IMMATURE WILL INHERIT THE EARTH

The more polarized a relationship is by traditional role playing, the greater the urgency to have children in order to give the relationship meaning, structure, and substance. The essentially empty interaction between the active, aggressive, emotionally distant male and the passive, identityless, childlike, madonna female *demands* to be filled up by having children early.

Dr. Bernice Lott tested the attitudes toward parenting of 289 male and female undergraduates at the University of Rhode Island. She found that the women who most wanted children were self-protective, fearful of danger, risk avoiding, inflexible, and incurious. "Who do we find planning to have children and desiring to rear them? Not those who would make the best mothers, but those with the least desirable characteristics," she concluded.[9]

Two members of the Department of Child Development and Family Relations at Texas Tech queried husbands about their desire to have children. They chose a random sample of 342 unmarried college men to fill out a questionnaire on how many children they would want under a variety of circumstances. According to the results, the young men

wanted fewer offspring when the husband-wife relationship was more egalitarian. When they imagined
that the women they married wanted no children, the
men seemed willing to go along with that decision.[10]

The Institute of Social Research at the University
of Michigan explored the question of why couples
choose parenthood, with 1,569 married women aged
fifteen to thirty-nine years old. They found that
"larger families were desired by those mothers who
counted 'having something useful to do' as one ad-
vantage of having children—a response which came
more often from mothers without jobs."[11]

It is unlikely that we could find healthy, self-
caring, nondefensive motivations for young people
to have a large number of children. Parenting in that
way creates and perpetuates the vicious cycle of
frustrated, ambivalent parents, and children who do
not really feel loved or cared about and who grow
up with an impaired capacity to feel good about
themselves, to love others, and to be healthy parents themselves. The contemporary breakdown of
family life, I believe, is the final result of the
immature, unhealthy parenting that eventually made
the family experience for many people more a trauma
than a positive experience they would wish to repeat.
Indeed, it is difficult to find people who say that
they want to have a relationship like their parents'
or want a family for themselves like the one they
came from.

LATE PARENTING AND THE NEW MALE-FEMALE RELATIONSHIP

As parenting becomes a conscious rather than a
defensive and automatic choice, it will increasingly
come at a time in life when having a child is an

enhancement and an organic expression of one's own fulfilled and secure identity. Therefore, it will be relatively stressless parenting in that it will be chosen at a time in both parents' lives when nothing of critical importance is being sacrificed and there are no significant resistances, frustrations, or conflicts about it. *People will only have children when there is a passionate, conscious craving to be a parent.*

The movement toward later parenting has already begun among a small but significant group of women. These are women who have examined their motives and trusted their resistances to early, automatic mothering. They are having children at a time in their lives when the desire is conscious and powerful and they are prepared to engage in it with joyous enthusiasm.

A survey of women who became mothers after age thirty quoted a well-known natural childbirth advocate: "The maternal urge is far stronger in the older mother, especially if she has only a few years left to produce."[12]

A study by an Ohio State psychologist of older mothers with eight-month-old babies found the mothers to be more flexible and aware of the complexities of child care, and to offer their children more appropriate visual stimulation than younger mothers.[13]

The most compelling evidence comes from the mothers themselves: "They are almost always positive: despite the risks and hassles, they found the experience enriching. . . . In the midst of America's graying of motherhood, it is hard to find any graying mother who believes she made a mistake."[14]

The contention that older mothers face special health hazards was explored by one woman writer who concluded that "problems in pregnancy and childbirth are not so much dependent upon a woman's age as they are upon her health in general. The reason some older women (35 to 40 years or older) are considered 'high risk' is that they may also have high blood pressure, underworked muscles, or heart conditions. Or they may be overweight. Or they may have any one of a number of diseases—complicating the pregnancy. Or they may be drug dependent—alcohol, cigarettes, birth control pills or worse. Or they may have bad eating habits and be undernourished even though they have quite enough to eat."[15]

Research also suggests that men and women become more whole, and therefore better candidates for marriage and parenting, in middle age. Specifically, men become more capable of affiliation and closeness and women become more assertive.[16]

One thirty-seven-year-old first-time mother, a television news reporter, perhaps stated the case for later mothering best: "I already have an identity outside the home. I don't feel a child will cheat me out of anything. I am established and I'm not frightened that I'll lose my job."[17]

It is hard to believe that the delighted response of older mothers would not be matched by men postponing parenthood until they have put economic preoccupations, romantic and sexual fantasies, and the impulse to experiment into perspective, so that they would not feel cheated by fatherhood. At such a time, their energies would also be freed to develop the personal, human capacities that are necessary to fathering. Premature parenting has only destroyed the fathering experience—and in cases where divorce occurred, it has often devastated the rest of the man's life as well. Therefore, later parenting would not only facilitate a potentially joyous experience, but also prevent a tragically self-destructive alienation from family and home.

Corinne N. Nydegger of the Institute of Human Development at the University of California, Berkeley, published a study which concluded that "late fathers are great fathers." Older men are more comfortable and self-possessed than their counterparts who became parents in their twenties. They see their role as that of a living model for humanistic values. While young men want to mold their children in a specific way, older fathers want to help their children grow and develop autonomously. They are also more likely to compromise with their children, while early dads are more likely to impose decisions on them.[18]

NONSEXISM AND THE HOW-TOS OF CHILD REARING

Preoccupation with how-to techniques of child rearing, as an intellectualization of the process, often reflects underlying ambivalence and resistances that parents have denied but are the real causes of problem children. The parents attempt to remedy the problem by finding a correct way to handle the child, rather than examine their inner conflicts and underlying feelings of resentment, which more likely created the difficulty.

If intellectual knowledge were the key to successful child rearing, then professionals in the field—psychiatrists, psychologists, social workers—would be the most effective parents. More often, the children of these professionals suffer from endless mixed messages the parents communicate. Sophisticated intellectualizations are out of sync with deeper feelings and nonverbal messages. The children are starved for a spontaneous, clear, gut-level response. The absence of this seriously impairs the children's sense of reality and capacity to be close, trusting, and giving in their later adult relationships. Instead, they continue the pattern of intellectualizing every relationship as as unconscious way of keeping intimacy at a safe distance.

Some of the most disturbed and hostile children I have seen are children of educationally "perfect" parents, who have studied formal parenting techniques and have learned to give all the "correct" parenting responses. Every communication of theirs produces a conflict between the "perfect" words the child hears, and the vastly different feeling the child receives on nonverbal levels.

Children relate to the deep feelings they sense, rather than premeditated verbal and behavioral expressions. One young father described it aptly. Children, he write, "absorb unexpressed emotions, the context of words, the nonverbal communications that we may or may not be aware of ourselves, the hidden messages. They're like sponges. These messages fill them up and they carry all of it around—sometimes . . . it's a heavy load. If your children seem troubled, it might help to take a look at what you're asking them to carry. They'll give you back a very accurate reflection of yourself."[19]

The new parenting consciousness will recognize that *who* the parent is—the being, development, nondefensiveness, authenticity, and congruence of the mother or father—is what really affects the child. In that sense, the obsession with the how-to specifics of raising children in a nonsexist way will be seen as misplaced and defensive. Parents who desire to bring up a child in a liberated way best serve that child by doing the hard work of growing themselves first. Simply choosing the correct toys, literature, clothes, and television shows for the child is psychologically naïve and will prove futile.

Nonsexism in child rearing is primarily a matter of promoting the full development and self-expressiveness of the child; and children learn that by modeling themselves on their parents, nonverbally as well as verbally. Genuinely nonsexist parenting is parenting by two whole, balanced, non-gender-defensive people, rather than a self-conscious process using a new rigid list of shoulds, shouldn'ts, and how-tos.

This includes even the "enlightened" emphasis in contemporary literature on father's getting more involved in the parenting process. As an abstract idea, this seems wonderful. However, if such fathering is engaged in on a "should" or how-to basis, it can be more damaging than no fathering at all. Fathers need first to grow beyond their masculine defensiveness, so that no one will even need to suggest greater participation to them. Rather, they will have a spontaneous hunger for it. Until their resistances are acknowledged and genuinely worked through, the fathering will be forced, artificial, and double-binding. Those who blindly prod fathers to get involved, therefore, may be doing more harm than good, unless they recognize that healthy fathering first and foremost requires a nondefensive, whole, developed male.

In most matters of "how to," unless the techniques are perfectly congruent with one's emotional,

nonverbal messages, they can be far more damaging
than helpful. I concur with Dr. Heinz Kohut of the
Chicago Institute of Psychoanalysis, who commented,
"It doesn't count what parents do but what they
really are."[20]

PARENTING IN THE NEW MALE-FEMALE RELATIONSHIP

In the new male-female relationship, the couple
will have children at a time when the child can add
to the relationship without requiring any deeply felt
sacrifice. This will facilitate a fully loving response
by parents who are not in conflict over the child.
The presence of the child will allow the parents to
become freer still, and to expand themselves and
feel happier about their lives, rather than making
them more serious and compulsive.

Having a child will feel easy and right; there will
be no need to weigh the pros and cons of becoming
a parent. The relationship between the partners will
be intrinsically fulfilling and it will feel good being
together even without a child. Having the child,
therefore, will be an expression of the relationship
rather than a way to fill an empty interaction.

The parents will be at a point in their own development and awareness where they will be able to
relate confidently, secure in the awareness that a
genuine, expressive, nonintellectualized response
coming from a whole parent is the best and only
"technique" that is crucial. Role responsibility and
who should do what and when will not be major
issues. Such preoccupations would suggest that the
child is viewed primarily as a duty that one or both
fear being unfairly laden with, rather than a joy they
are ready and eager for.

There will be no concern over technically perfect parenting. Both parents will have a clearly defined, positive sense of themselves, so that they can relate to the child as a separate human being with its own needs, rather than as an extension of the parents' egos and images. In addition, the parents will have grown beyond concern over whether any form of human expression is appropriate to one particular sex. Thus they can allow their child to become fully human without pressure to be masculine or feminine.

In summary, passing the baton means that child rearing will be a benevolent trusteeship rather than a way of promoting the parents' interests. It will be nonintellectualized, with a maximum of authentic involvement and a minimum of how-tos. It is a matter of feeling so good about one's own fulfilled life that there will be no resentment toward the children for being and becoming whatever they emerge as, partially because the parents will have the child at a time when it can be the primary focus of their energy without creating the feeling of sacrifice.

The prime motivations for becoming a parent will be the "selfish" joy of the process itself and the opportunity to grow oneself as a result.

13   A Balanced Tomorrow

WITH THE ARRIVAL OF the new male-female relationship, the primary motivation for getting involved with another person will be mutual enrichment, facilitation, and enhancement. Men and women will choose each other because they *want* to be together, not because they *need* each other for security or self-validating reasons. That is, the relationship will be developed because it is intrinsically nourishing and stimulating, and not for reasons of concern about image or the future. Therefore, a man and a woman will be drawn together initially because of the good feelings they generate in each other, and not because of gender symbols such as his occupational status and earning power, or her physical proportions and potential to make him look good.

The new balanced relationship will reverse the

traditional relationship process, which transformed romance into resentment, harmony into bickering, early parenting into parent-child estrangement, feeling rescued into feeling trapped, excitement into boredom, being "best friends" into feelings of alienation, and the idealization of one's partner into revulsion, fear, or even hatred. Romance will not be attractive or addictive, while genuine knowing and playfulness will be paramount.

The male-female relationship will be put back on its feet, after traditional socialization stood it on its head and produced a regression in which the best came first and euphoria slowly gave way to frustration, fatigue, and resentment. Instead, the balanced relationship will involve steady progression, meaning a growing, increasingly flexible interaction between two people who are capable of continually recreating the relationship according to the changing realities of each other.

Each couple will custom-tailor their own structure, and not attempt to conform to prior models of "normal" or "adjusted" relationships. This will come from an awareness that all formal models of the past were the products of various defensive distortions and are unnecessary for couples who are aware and trusting of their sensibilities. This will also give the relationship the capacity to continually absorb new information and remake itself according to the changing needs of the partners.

The balanced new consciousness, therefore, will be an original creation of the relationship, rather than the melding of masculine and feminine prerogatives and characteristics, which would only produce the sum of two distorted postures. In other words, the balanced relationship will be a unique entity, not merely the result of making traditional masculine and feminine compulsions available to both.

Concerns over what is normal and abnormal in the relationship will recede. Instead, all behavior will be seen as a personal statement, and reacted to according to its impact and what it expresses about the relationship.

Role playing, rituals, and religious expression will be creative and expressive outgrowths of the relationship, not external structures that define or constrain it.

Materialism will enhance but not dominate the relationship, nor will it be a primary preoccupation. Both partners will have a sense of security and competence about their capacity to provide for themselves. Emphasis on acquisition in the relationship will be seen as reflecting personal deadness, defensiveness, lack of playfulness and the disguising of bordeom and resentment.

Total and comfortable expressiveness, relaxed openness, nonintellectualized interchanges, and an energy-generating playfulness will characterize the flow of the relationship. There will be a minimum of seriousness and weighty intellectualizing about issues, and a maximum of spontaneous, playful, and creative interplay.

Both partners will feel comfortable and capable of the full expression of any part of themselves, and a nonsexist interaction will be a direct and natural outgrowth of this nondefensiveness. Consequently, the expression of any needs, emotions, or behaviors will never be judged in terms of appropriateness for a man or woman.

Sexism will be seen as symptomatic of gender

defensiveness, rather than being viewed as an objective ideological issue. Therefore, preoccupation with it will be seen as a reflection of the disturbance of the relationship itself, rather than as a matter for negotiation, argument, and intellectualization.

Giving and loving will be a response to the true needs of one's partner, rather than the product of the partners' need to validate their own images of themselves, disguised as caring and sharing.

Intimacy, understanding, and closeness will be an effortless consequence of the wholeness of the two people in this balanced relationship, and will be possible to the extent that such a state exists. It will not have to be worked at in a premeditated way.

Enduring, committed relationships will preferably be entered into only after one has grown to become a whole person, rather than using the relationship as a vehicle for growth. The more polarized or lacking in wholeness the traditional couple is, the more they tend to choose each other for defensive reasons, and thus be resistant to, rather than facilitative of, each other's growth. Therefore, when change does take place, it is in defiant reaction against one's partner, rather than for the benefit of the relationship.

Being fully known and exposed will be a key component of the relationship, with each person cherishing the other person's self-exposure and his or her own. Feelings of loneliness and isolation will be absent because one's true self will be known and appreciated by the other.

The wholeness of each partner, rather than the destruction of real differences, will be seen. Indeed, the balanced relationship will finally make it possible to determine what the genuine differences between men and women, rather than the defensively derived ones, really are—if any, in fact, exist.

Both men and women will be able to see the world accurately and undistorted. The man will be free of the masculine filters that have in the past put him in constant combat with self-created pressures, creating in him a compulsion to triumph and gain power in order to be "loved." Likewise, the woman will no longer view the world distorted by her feminine defenses, which have caused her to seek shelter and identity through the man's warrior posture.

He will be free of compulsive, proving behavior in relating to her, and she will not be stunted by fear that displaying strength, autonomy, assertion, or sexuality will detract from her attractiveness as a woman.

The nourishing quality of the relationship will be expressed, in part, by the absence of depression, escape through alcohol or drugs, severe anxiety, and other symptoms of the repression of important parts of a person's self.

Being together at any given time will be the result of a consciously made decision, rather than an automatic act that is the product of defensive fusion and the fear of setting honest boundaries and limits.

Concern over growth and personal development, rather than over adjustment and appropriateness, will characterize the healthy, balanced, new interaction.

Both partners will expand in terms of their interests, attitudes, responses, passions, and capacities for experiencing and enjoying life. The experience created by the relationship will be greater than what either could experience separately.

Stability, in the best sense of the word, will be

present, meaning that both will be conscious masters of the nature and direction of the relationship, not the victims of its unexpected turns. A steadiness that is not rigidity or blandness, but simply the product of a consciousness that prevents the defensive roller coaster of sudden euphoria and shattering lows, will characterize the course of the relationship. The partners will be free of painful, unexpected twists in their separate lives as well. Experiences such as the "mid-life crisis" will be seen as artifacts of the defensive consciousness of the sexes that previously caused abrupt eruptions of their denied selves.

Each partner will be sensitive to the reciprocal nature of the relationship experience and how it reinforces and perpetuates the responses of the other. In that sense, they will recognize how they get what they "deserve" or are ready for. Changing the relationship will therefore involve changing the reactions in oneself that allow for the other person's behavior, rather than attempting to change the other person directly.

Conflicts will be viewed as the products of a two-way relationship process, and resolved from the vantage points of two partners focusing on their own contributions to it, both willing to change in order to improve it. There will be no assigning fault, placing blame, or laying guilt. Nor will there be a desire on one person's part to analyze or change the other person as a "solution" to the problem.

Problems will be handled by honest confrontation, plus a sensitivity to and exposure of underlying feelings, rather than by the use of techniques and how-tos supposedly designed to create a certain effect through external manipulation, strategy, or "treatment."

The expression of resistances, limits, and anger and the negotiation of conflict will be welcomed as a positive and necessary dimension, equal in importance to expressions of love, mutuality, and understanding. This will prevent any buildup of hidden rage. Therefore, no mean or destructive exchanges will take place.

There will be a slow, progressive movement through conflict, and an acknowledgment of boundaries and resistances toward intimacy. Thus, the relationship will get closer and more flexible with time, rather than decline in closeness, regardless of whether the marriage itself lasts.

Physical health and awareness of the body will be positively affected by the new gender-free consciousness. This will result from stopping the distorting of the body's experiences by gender defenses—specifically, the use of illness as an expression of repressed emotions or needs; the denial of or excessive emphasis on pain, fatigue, or need for help because of masculine and feminine conditioning; or diet choices based on their appropriateness for men or women.

Sexuality in the balanced relationship will not be defined or encumbered by performance expectations, or any other preconceived standards. Sexual experience will be recognized as an extension and expression of the separate individuals involved and the relationship itself. These experiences will, therefore, constantly vary in quality and quantity, and will be viewed as statements of where each person and the relationship are, rather than as problems or symptoms. The "tyranny of sexuality" with its focus on statistics, labels of dysfunction, and fabricated definitions of normality will disappear naturally.

Work, childbearing, and parenting may be significant expressions of the relationship, but will be just a few aspects among many others, not its central purposes.

Birth control concerns will be constructively handled as the natural result of a relationship between two self-caring people who recoil from premature parenting, which would impede their growth, personal development, and exploration of fantasies and pleasures. Children will be conceived only when they enhance their parents' lives and so will not be viewed as a heavy burden or responsibility.

In general, antagonism between the sexes will be remembered as a fossil from a primitive state of male-female consciousness that grew painfully out of our masculine and feminine conditioning and made victims and enemies of the men and women involved. The balanced, new male-female relationship will be defined by conscious, nondefensive, self-caring interaction between a man and a woman who are both fully capable of experiencing, expressing, and acting on the whole range of their human needs, emotions, impulses, strengths, and potentials. The relationship will be known by its process, and by its rootedness in the here-and-now reality of two people who are delighted and enhanced by one another.

Notes

CHAPTER 1

1. Ted Turner in Studs Terkel, *American Dreams* (New York: Pantheon Books, 1980), pp. 67–68.

2. Lee Hotz, "Asbestos Workers Find Payoff Is Disease, Death," *The Pittsburgh Press*, March 30, 1980, Section C, p. 1.

3. Bernard Lefkowitz, "Life Without Work," *Newsweek*, May 14, 1979, p. 31.

4. Una Stannard, "The Mask of Beauty," in *Woman in Sexist Society*, ed. by Vivian Gornick and Barbara K. Moran (New York: New American Library, 1971), p. 203.

5. Libby Severinghaus Warner, "Clare Boothe Luce Talks About Women and Success," *Bulletin of the Baldwin School*, Vol. 40, No. 5 (Sept. 1974), p. 1.

6. Pamela Butler, *Self-Assertion for Women: A*

Guide to Becoming Androgynous (San Francisco: Canfield Press, 1976), p. 5.

7. Joseph J. Jaffa, letter to the editor, *Newsweek*, April 17, 1978, p. 8.

8. Evelyn P. Stevens, "Machismo and Marianismo," *Society*, Vol 10 (Sept. –Oct. 1973), p. 58.

9. Sandra Lipsitz Bem, "Androgeny vs. the Tight Little Lives of Fluffy Women and Chesty Men," *Psychology Today*, Sept. 1975, p. 9.

10. J. Conrad Schwarz, "Childhood Origins of Psychopathology," *American Psychologist*, Vol. 34, No. 10 (Oct. 1979), p. 880.

11. Ibid.

12. Peter A. Martin, *A Marital Therapy Manual* (New York: Brunner/Mazel, 1976), pp. 16–17.

13. Sylvia Plath, *The Bell Jar* (New York: Bantam Books, 1975), p. 58.

14. Ibid., p. 67.

15. William Goode, *A Staff Report to the National Commission on the Causes and Prevention of Violence*, ed. by Donald J. Mulvihill and Melvin M. Tumin (Washington, D.C.: U.S. Government Printing Office, 1969), Vol. 13, Appendix 19.

CHAPTER 2

1. Karen Coleman and Paula Howard, "Conjugal Violence: What the Women Report," a paper presented at a meeting of the American Psychological Association in Toronto, 1978.

2. Bruce J. Rounsaville, "Theories in Marital Violence: Evidence From a Study of Battered Women," *Victimology*, Vol. 3, 1–2 (1978), pp. 11–31.

3. Barbara Star, "Comparing Battered and Non-Battered Women," *Victimology*, Vol. 3, 1–2 (1978), pp. 32–44.

4. Joseph N. Bell, "Rescuing the Battered Wife," *Human Behavior*, June 1977, pp. 16–23.

5. *Behavior Today: The Professional's Newsletter*, Vol. 10, No. 24 (June 25, 1979), pp. 5–6.

6. Murray A. Straus, "Wife Beating: How Common and Why?," *Victimology*, Vol. 2, 3–4 (1977–1978), pp. 443–58.

7. Paul Dean, "Male Suffering in Silence: The Battered-Husband Syndrome," *View, Los Angeles Times*, Nov. 14, 1980, p. 1.

CHAPTER 3

1. Doug Smith, "Unhappy: 50 Years Together Doesn't Prove Marriage Is Golden," *Minneapolis Star*, July 21, 1980, p. 1B.

2. "Life Without the Tube," *Time*, April 10, 1972, p. 47.

3. Howard Rosenberg, "Strike Fails to Dim T.V. Watching," *Los Angeles Times*, November 5, 1980, Part VI, p. 9.

4. C. N. Parkinson, *Parkinson's Law and Other Studies in Administration* (Boston: Houghton Mifflin Co., 1957), p. 2.

5. Walter R. Nord and Robert Costigan, "Worker Adjustment to the Four-Day Week: A Longitudinal Study," *Journal of Applied Psychology*, Vol. 58, No. 1, pp. 60–66.

6. Anita Bryant, *Mine Eyes Have Seen the Glory* (Old Tappen, N.J.: Fleming H. Revell Co., 1970), p. 84.

7. Anita Bryant, *Bless This House* (New York: Bantam Books, 1976), pp. 51–52.

8. Marabel Morgan, *The Total Woman* (New York: Pocket Books, 1975), p. 8.

9. Sally Quinn, "A Visit With Mr. and Mrs. 'Total Woman,' " *Los Angeles Times*, Feb. 19, 1978, Part VIII, p. 10.

10. Ruth Carter Stapleton, *The Gift of Inner Healing* (Watts, Tex.: World Books, 1976), p. 18.

11. Ibid., p. 32.

12. Kenneth S. Lynn, "The Strange Unhappy Life of Max Perkins," *Commentary*, Vol. 66, No. 6 (Dec. 1978), p. 61.

CHAPTER 4

1. *Newsletter* (Masters and Johnson Institute), Vol. 2, No. 1 (Feb. 1981), p. 4.

2. Ellen Frank, Carol Anderson, and Debra Rubinstein, "Frequency of Sexual Dysfunction in Normal Couples," *New England Journal of Medicine*, Vol. 299, 3 (July 1978), pp. 111–15.

3. L. Rainwater, "Sexual and Marital Relations," in *Family Design* (Chicago: Aldine Publishing Co., 1965), p. 83.

4. Ibid., p. 113.

5. William H. Masters and Virginia Johnson, *Homosexuality in Perspective* (Boston: Little, Brown and Co., 1979).

6. Shere Hite, *The Hite Report: A Nationwide Study of Female Sexuality* (New York: Macmillan Publishing Co., 1976).

7. Helen Singer Kaplan, *Disorders of Sexual Desire and Other New Concepts and Techniques in Sex Therapy* (New York: Brunner/Mazel, 1979).

8. "Medicine: The Sex-Therapy Revolution," *Newsweek*, Nov. 17, 1980, p. 98.

9. Arthur Bell, "Asexual Chic: Everybody's Not Doing It," *The Village Voice*, Jan. 23, 1978, pp. 20–21.

10. Richard A. Silverman, "Lysistrata, Mon Amour, Mon Amour," *The Village Voice*, May 2, 1974, p. 106.

CHAPTER 5

1. T. L. and M. S. Gove Nichols, *Marriage: Its History, Character and Results; Its Sanctities and Its Profanities; Its Science and Its Facts* (Cincinnati: 1854), p. 20, passim.

2. W. A. Alcott, *The Young Woman's Guide to Excellence* (New York: 1846), pp. 295–99.

3. Colette Dowling, "Beyond Liberation: Confessions of a Dependent Woman," *New York*, Aug. 8, 1977, p. 32.

4. Ibid., p. 34.

5. Jean Callahan, "Why Are All Marriages Breaking Up," *Mother Jones*, July 1977, pp. 19–24.

6. Peggy Taylor, "Why Marry," *New Age*, July 1979, pp. 30–32.

7. Helen Z. Lopata, "Living Through Widowhood," *Psychology Today*, July 1973, p. 88.

8. Hugh Drummond, "Diagnosing Marriage," *Mother Jones*, July 1979, p. 20.

9. Peter J. Stein, "Singlehood: An Alternative to Marriage," *The Family Coordinator*, October 1975, p. 493.

10. Ibid., p. 489.

CHAPTER 6

1. Phyllis Raphael, "So Sane—and Going Crazy," *The Village Voice*, Oct. 20, 1975, p. 55.

2. Lee Eisenberg, "Looking for a Wife," *Esquire*, Dec. 1980, p. 30.

3. "The Superwoman Squeeze," *Newsweek*, May 19, 1980, p. 74.

4. Marcia Seligson, "Author and Her Subjects Bare Souls in 'A Different Woman' " *Los Angeles Times Calendar*, Dec. 16, 1973, p. 82.

5. Karen Durbin, "A Woman Talks About Her Identity," *Mademoiselle*, July 1972, p. 162.

6. "The War Between the Sexes: Is It Manufactured or Real?," *Ebony*, June 1979, p. 38.

7. Ibid., p. 39.

CHAPTER 7

1. Carolyn G. Heilbrun, *Reinventing Womanhood* (New York: W. W. Norton and Co., 1979), p. 95.

2. A. A. Lazarus, ed., *Clinical Behavior Therapy* (New York: Brunner/Mazel, 1972), p. 34.

3. Frances-Dee Burlin and Roberta A. Guzzetta, "Existentialism: Toward a Theory of Psychotherapy for Women," *Psychotherapy: Theory, Research and Practice*, Vol. 14, No. 3 (Fall 1977), pp. 264–65.

4. Andrea Chambers, "Witty, Raunchy and No-body's Eunuch, Germaine Greer Is Teaching Tulsa a Thing or Two," *People*, Dec. 17, 1979, p. 102.

5. J. David Truby, "Women of Violence," *West Coast Review of Books*, Vol. 5, No. 2, pp. 64–72.

6. Ibid.

7. Jeffrey E. Kantor, Bart E. Noble, Sandra A. Leisey, and Terry McFarlane, "Air Force Female Pilots Program: Initial Performance and Attitudes," *U.S. AFHRL Technical Report*, No. 78-67 (Feb. 1979), p. 38.

8. Geoffrey Norman, "Out of the Frying Pan, Into the Fire," *Rolling Stone*, Nov. 17, 1972, p. 46.

9. Berkeley Rice, "Midlife Encounters: The Men-

ninger Seminars for Businessmen," *Psychology Today,* April 19/9, p. 96.

10. Tim Fay (interview) in "Men's Group Members Talk About Their Experiences," *Free Men's Options: The Men's Liberation Newsletter,* Oct.–Nov. 1980, p. 3.

11. Lanny Kutakoff, "Looking at the Last Men's Sharing Day," *Men Sharing* No. 2 (June 1975), p. 3.

CHAPTER 9

1. P. H. Klopfer, "Sensory Physiology and Aesthetics," *American Scientist,* 58 (1970), pp. 399–403.

2. K. Lorenz, "Plays and Vacuum Activities," in *L'Instinct Doux: Le Comportement des Animaux et de L'homme,* ed. by M. Antouri et al. (Paris: Masson, 1956), and K. Lorenz, *King Solomon's Ring* (New York: New American Library, 1972), described in Brian Vandenbert, "Play and Development From an Ethological Perspective," *American Psychologist,* Vol. 33, No. 8 (August, 1978), p. 733.

3. Arthur Koestler, *The Act of Creation* (New York: Macmillan Co., 1964), p. 510.

4. Eric Plaut, "Play and Adaptation," *Psychoanalytic Study of the Child,* Vol. 34 (1979), pp. 217–232.

5. K. Sylva, J. Bruner, and P. Genova, "The Role of Play in the Problem Solving of Children 3–5 Years Old," in *Play,* ed. by J. Bruner, A. Jolly, and K. Sylva (New York: Basic Books, 1976), p. 244.

6. Barbara Lusk Forisha, *Sex Roles and Personal Awareness* (Morristown, N.J.: General Learning Press, 1978), p. 87.

7. Mihaly Csikszentmihalyi, *Beyond Boredom and Anxiety* (San Francisco: Jossey-Bass, 1975), pp. 36–42, 47.

8. Michael Novak, *The Joy of Sports: End Zones, Bases, Baskets, Balls and the Consecration of the American Spirit* (New York: Basic Books, 1976), p. 40.

CHAPTER 10

1. Linda Bird Francke, "Executive Heart-Hunters," *New York*, Feb. 16, 1981, pp. 44–45.
2. Linda Wolfe, "Love and Work: How to Succeed," *New York*, Feb. 16, 1981, p. 31.
3. Honora Lee Wolfe, "Desert Dance," *New Age*, Vol. 4, No. 8 (Feb. 1979), p. 19.

CHAPTER 11

1. Betty Dodson, "Getting to Know Me," *Ms.*, Vol. III, No. 2 (August 1974), p. 107.
2. Julia Heiman, Leslie LoPiccolo, and Joseph LoPiccolo, *Becoming Orgasmic: A Sexual Growth Program for Women* (Englewood Cliffs, N.J.: Prentice-Hall, 1976).
3. Mary Jane Sherfey, *The Nature and Evolution of Female Sexuality* (New York: Random House, 1972).
4. John B. Sisk, "Sexual Stereotypes," *Commentary*, Vol. 64, No. 14 (Oct. 1977), p. 59.
5. Daisy Hilse Dwyer, *Images and Self-images: Male and Female in Morocco* (New York: Columbia University Press, 1978).
6. Michael Adam, *Wandering in Eden: Three Ways to the East Within Us* (New York: Alfred A. Knopf, 1976), p. 15.
7. Dio Urmilla Neff, "The Way of Love," *Yoga Journal*, May 1981, p. 10.

CHAPTER 12

1. Donald McDonald, "The Liberation of Women," *The Center Magazine: A Publication of the Center for the Study of Democratic Institutions*, Vol. 5, No. 3 (May–June 1972), p. 30.

2. Hans Sebald, *Momism: The Silent Disease of America* (Chicago: Nelson-Hall, 1976).

3. Evelyn P. Stevens, "Machismo and Marianismo," *Society*, Vol. 10 (Sept.–Oct. 1973), p. 63.

4. Elizabeth Stone, "Mothers and Daughters: Taking a New Look at Mom," *The New York Times Magazine*, May 13, 1979, p. 62.

5. Ibid.

6. Richard J. Gelles, "Violence Toward Children in the United States," *American Journal of Orthopsychiatry*, Vol. 48, 4 (Oct. 1978), pp. 580–92.

7. George Alexander, "Motherhood Called Less Than Joy," *Los Angeles Times*, Nov. 18, 1977, Part I, p. 3.

8. Karen S. Renne, "Childlessness, Health and Marital Satisfaction," *Social Biology*, Vol. 23, 3 (Fall 1976), pp. 183–97.

9. Bernice E. Lott, "Who Wants the Children? Some Relationships Among Attitudes Toward Children, Parents and the Liberation of Women," *American Psychologist*, Vol. 28, No. 7 (July 1973), pp. 573–82.

10. Jan E. Harrell and Nancy McCunney, "The Couple Relationship as a Predictor of Desired Family Size," a paper presented at a meeting of the American Psychological Association in San Francisco, 1977.

11. Lois Hoffman and Jean Manis, "Why Couples Choose Parenthood," *ISR Newsletter* (Institute for

Social Research, University of Michigan), Autumn 1978, p. 7.

12. Linda Bird Francke, Mary Hager, and Lisa Whitman, "A Baby After 30," *Newsweek*, Nov. 13, 1978, pp. 128–29.

13. Ibid., p. 129.

14. Ibid.

15. Paula L. Cizmar, "Aunt Mary Said There'd Be Days Like This," *Mother Jones*, Vol. 4, No. 2 (Feb.– Mar. 1979), p. 28.

16. Henry Grunebaum, "Middle Age and Marriage: Affiliative Men and Assertive Women," *American Journal of Family Therapy*, Vol. 7, 3 (Fall 1979), pp. 46–50.

17. Lynn Langway, Diane Weathers, Sharon Walters, and Mary Hager, "At Long Last Motherhood," *Newsweek*, Mar. 16, 1981, p. 86D.

18. C. N. Nydegger, "The Older the Father: Late Is Great," *Psychology Today*, Apr. 1974, pp. 26–28.

19. Richard Warren Eivers, "Fathering in the 80's," *New Age*, June 1981, p. 36.

20. Giovanna Breu, "Medics," *People*, Feb. 26, 1979, p. 63.

Index

ABOUT THE AUTHOR

Herb Goldberg received his Ph.D. in clinical psychology from Adelphi University. He has been on the faculty of California State University since 1965, where he is presently Professor of Psychology. In addition, he has had a private practice with individuals, couples and families for over ten years and conducts workshops across the country. He is a contributor to numerous professional publications and the author of several books, including *The Hazards of Being Male* and *The New Male*, available in Signet editions.